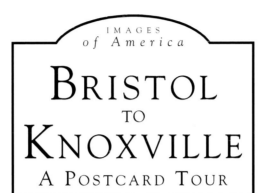

IMAGES
of America

BRISTOL
TO
KNOXVILLE
A POSTCARD TOUR

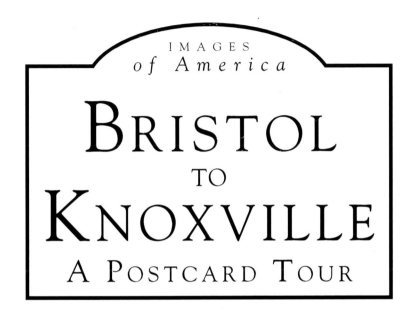

IMAGES
of America

BRISTOL
TO
KNOXVILLE
A POSTCARD TOUR

Elena Irish Zimmerman

ARCADIA
PUBLISHING

Published by Arcadia Publishing
Charleston, South Carolina

Printed in the United States of America

Library of Congress Catalog Card Number: Applied for

For all general information contact Arcadia Publishing at:
Telephone 843-853-2070
Fax 843-853-0044
E-mail sales@arcadiapublishing.com
For customer service and orders:
Toll-Free 1-888-313-2665

Visit us on the Internet at www.arcadiapublishing.com

This book is for Karl and Janice
who give me love and stability

Contents

ACKNOWLEDGMENTS

The author wishes to thank Betty Curtis, Paul Garland, and C. Milton Hinshilwood for their interest and advice concerning this book. Special thanks go to Paul Garland for the loan of postcards from his collection. Others who helped more than they know with their enthusiasm and support are members of the East Tennessee Postcard Club.

The author is grateful, too, for the permission to use pictures photographed by renowned photographers J.M. Thompson and W.M. Cline. Without these images, the book would not have been possible.

INTRODUCTION

Before we start our journey, let's consider what we are doing and where we are going.

This book features picture postcard images of East Tennessee towns as they appeared sixty or more years ago. We have climbed aboard our good old 1937 Ford and are prepared to set out on a little journey up and down the highways of East Tennessee, visiting briefly in the towns we encounter on the way. It is the year 1939. There is much, much that the present world knows that the world of 1939 did not know, and this knowledge will not, for the most part, appear here. World War II had not yet happened; Oak Ridge and the atomic bomb did not exist; we did not know television, videos, computers, microwaves, or anything else of electronic technology. We were unaware of the coming social problems of drug addiction, AIDS, and homelessness. Free love and women's rights were in very low profile. We did not have the interstate system, gigantic superstores, or polyester clothing. Even though we did have other problems—notably the Great Depression—it would seem that we were relatively innocent.

We are going to pretend, then, that we are back in 1939, and that our family has the vacation time to set out to see East Tennessee. We will start from the state line and drive down one of the principal highways of the time. As we visit various towns or experience events along the way, we will reflect briefly on the history and relevant facts that emerge, and our postcard pictures will illustrate much of what we see.

We must make a note that East Tennessee is defined here as that portion of the state included east of a line drawn on the map from South Pittsburg in Marion County north to Byrdstown in Pickett County. Our tour visits but a small part of this area, and the towns selected are but a few of the total number on the map. Not all towns have been photographed for postcards, and from the ones which were, those chosen for this book seemed to be the most important.

This book does not offer a definitive history of the communities covered, for it is a historical scenic drive rather than a history in the academic sense. Efforts have been made, however, to verify facts and to be as accurate as possible. If a postcard was mailed, the date is given, and usually the message is quoted as well. Most messages on postcards are rather trivial, though sometimes quite revealing; we read, "Hello, how are you, haven't heard from you" or "Beautiful scenery here, had a nice trip. Will be home Sunday" and the like. Sometimes there is a comment illuminating the view pictured; sometimes the card has printed information on the back describing or explaining the view. Where the messages on mailed cards are quoted, the language of the sender is left in its original form.

Some of the best photographic history of early-twentieth-century America lies in postcards published between 1900 and 1940, and some of the most significant details of our social history can be inferred from their brief messages. This book came about because of the extensive collection of vintage Tennessee postcards which were available, and because the author wants to share them with all those people who are interested in Tennessee life as it was during those years.

So—come with us and enjoy East Tennessee as it looked in days gone by. It was a good time to live here—as any time is—but it was a quieter time that some of us may not know and others may not remember. Our tour begins at the state line between Tennessee and Virginia.

One

BRISTOL
Sullivan County

We begin our tour in downtown Bristol. The city is composed of two municipalities: Bristol, TN, and Bristol, VA. The state line divides State Street, the main thoroughfare. This is a trading town and a railroad junction, complete with railroad yards and factories which produce pulp and paper, leather goods, mine cars, furniture, and structural steel. It is a shipping point for much of the farm produce of upper East Tennessee.

The original site of Bristol was a large Cherokee village known as "Camp Big Meet." In the 1750s it was known as Sapling Grove, and tracts of land were sold to James Patten, Evan Shelby, and Isaac Baker. In the 1830s Reverend James King, Jr., acquired the property, and in 1852 Joseph R. Anderson, Reverend King's son-in-law, purchased 100 acres of meadowland and named his development Bristol, after the port city in England.

In 1868 King's College for ministerial students (named for James King) was chartered by the Holston Presbytery to provide "a thorough classical and scientific training combined with moral and religious instruction." Located on 60 acres, the campus is landscaped with towering beech trees and much dogwood and evergreen. A quadrangle of seven brick buildings was formed in 1917; they are the work of C.B. Kearfort of Bristol and have a modified Georgian design.

Sullins College for young ladies also opened in 1868. It began as a private, two-year college. After being destroyed by fire in 1915, it was rebuilt and reopened in September 1917 with 227 students. The school catalog indicated that students might experience "meals, boarding, instruction, washing, and the attention of servants" for $160 per year. During the 1920s and 1930s the college continued to flourish. In 1976 the college closed abruptly because of financial problems, and the college property was sold to the United Coal Company. Sullins Academy, started in 1966 by the Reverend Charles A. Bledsoe as the Episcopal Day School, later took over the facility of the old Sullins College, where it continues today.   By 1887 Bristol was the largest and one of the most enterprising towns in East Tennessee. In 1890 the Tennessee legislature recognized the center of Main Street as the state line, and in 1902 the street's name was changed to State Street. The big sign now over State Street was erected in 1910 on top of the hardware building near the railroad tracks at the corner of Third and State Streets.

Bristol is surrounded by tremendous natural beauty and history. To the east of the city lies the upper section of the Cherokee National Forest, comprising 744,427 acres. On US 11E, 16 3/4 miles southwest of Bristol, stands a marker calling attention to Rocky Mount, one of the oldest houses in Tennessee. Located at Piney Flats, 4 miles north of Johnson City, the large log house was built by William Cobb in 1770 and is the oldest original territorial capitol in the United States. It became capitol of the territory south of the River Ohio in 1790, when President George Washington appointed William Blount Territorial Governor and Superintendent of Indian Affairs. Blount made his home with the Cobb family and conducted affairs of state from Rocky Mount until a new capitol was built at Knoxville in 1792. The two-and-a-half-story house is roofed with pegged white-oak shingles and has a large outside chimney made of home-pressed brick. The garden to the right of the house still contains lilies, roses, violets, and japonicas.

The journey from Bristol to Knoxville is 131.8 miles, traveling south on US 11E. The northern section of 11E follows the valley of upper East Tennessee, the route over which westward-moving wagon trains of the pioneers passed. We will now follow 11E to the junction with Route 19, which we will then take south to Elizabethton.

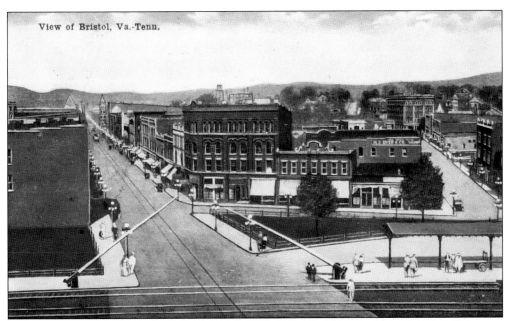

View of Bristol, Va.-Tenn.

View of Bristol, Va.-Tenn. Bristol is situated on the state line between Tennessee and Virginia and the city's Main Street is the dividing line between the states. The message on this card from 1920 reads: "How are you and husband. I hope improving rapidly. Came over to Bristol yesterday going home tomorrow. It took all the money I had to buy me a suit."

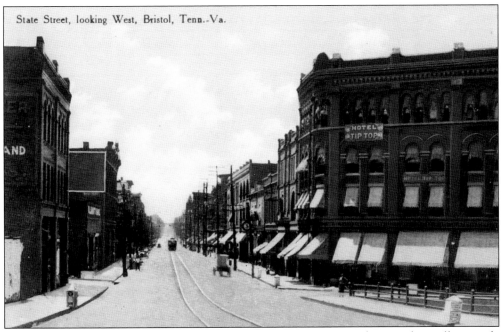

State Street, looking West, Bristol, Tenn.-Va.

State Street, looking West, Bristol, Tenn.-Va. A quiet street greets us here, with a trolley astride the state line in the background. The sender, in 1908, remarked: "Arrived safely in this city and have settled down to business. Think I will like it here fine."

11

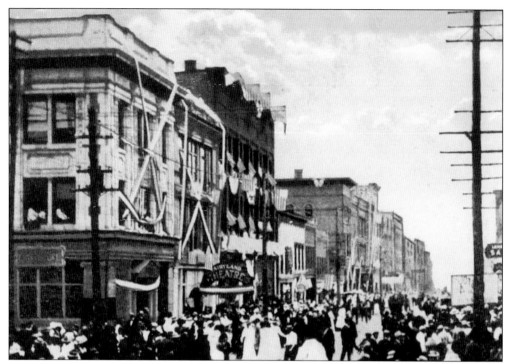

State Street, Bristol, Tenn. Three decades later this card was sent: "Hello sis everything is allright dont worry I am going down South again. Everything is lovely and the Goose hangs high faint heart never won fair lady or fat turkey—so here I am a Gispsy (sic) again—dont worry. Will."

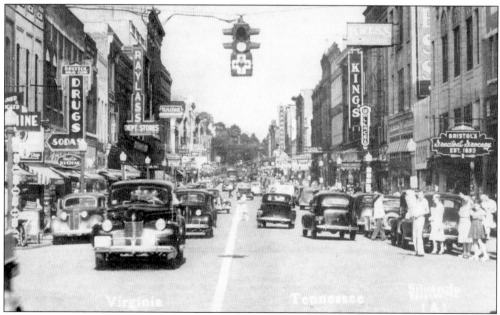

State Street. This wartime card shows Bristol's dividing line clearly marked, and early 1940s automobiles filling the street. The serviceman sender says: "Few Minutes layover here. Had coffee and doughnuts."

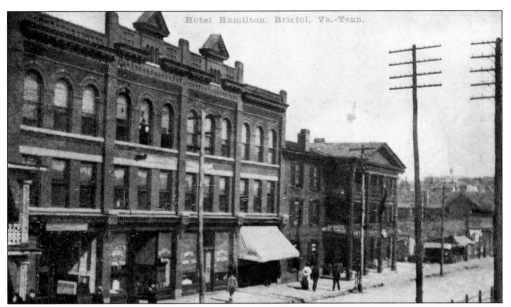

Hotel Hamilton, Bristol, Tenn. Hotels were generally modest structures in 1911, when this card was sent. The message reads: "Hello . . . I am away down in the sunny South this lonesome eve would like to see you I wrote you several letters but received no answers."

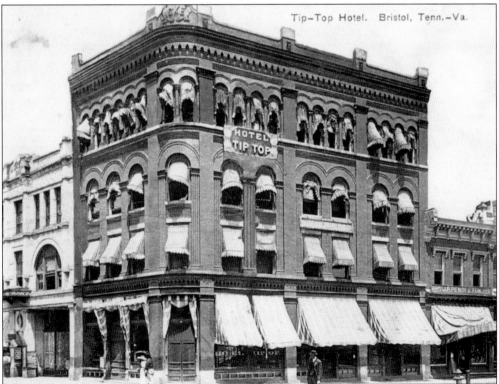

The Tip-Top Hotel, Bristol, Tenn. The sender seems to have enjoyed her stay here, about 1912: "Dear Martha, How do you like the looks of this hotel? . . . I have had such a good time. We were on the 4th floor last night—it was full to the Tip-Top."

13

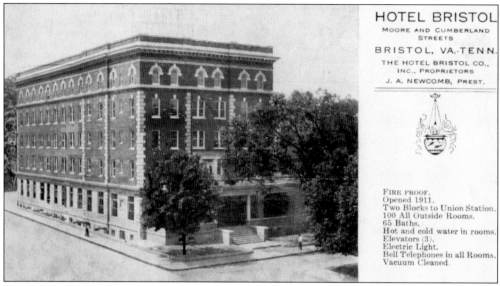

HOTEL BRISTOL
MOORE AND CUMBERLAND
STREETS
BRISTOL, VA.-TENN.
THE HOTEL BRISTOL CO.,
INC., PROPRIETORS
J. A. NEWCOMB, PREST.

FIRE PROOF.
Opened 1911.
Two Blocks to Union Station.
100 All Outside Rooms.
65 Baths.
Hot and cold water in rooms.
Elevators (3).
Electric Light.
Bell Telephones in all Rooms.
Vacuum Cleaned.

Hotel Bristol. A typical hotel advertising postcard presents the information and amenities next to the picture. The sender remarks: "Stayed here when we went to Bristol until our furniture came."

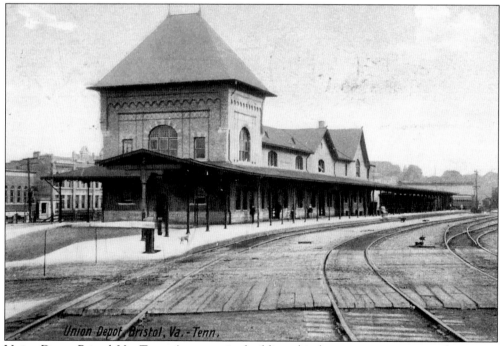

Union Depot, Bristol, Va.-Tenn.

Union Depot, Bristol, Va.-Tenn. An attractive building, this depot was convenient to downtown and the hotels. The card was mailed in 1908, and the sender informs the recipient: "This is the station I got off at this a.m. It is not near as pretty as the one at Brockton, Mass."

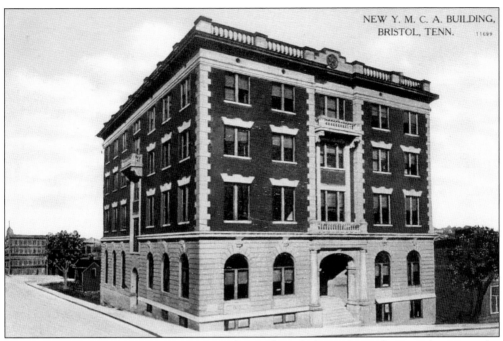

The New YMCA Building, Bristol, Tenn. This card, mailed in 1909, makes no reference to the Virginia half of the city. The sender says briefly: "I would have written you but I have been <u>very</u> ill. Am getting well, and am out of danger now, I think. Write to me soon."

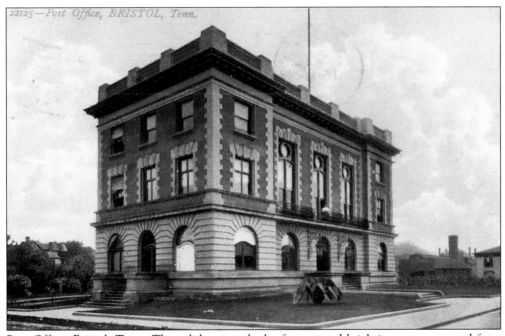

22125—Post Office, BRISTOL, Tenn.

Post Office, Bristol, Tenn. The solid, square look of stone and brick is once more used for a public building. The message on this card, mailed in 1909, reads: "Your postal received. I was sorry not to see you but had very little time. There is absolutely nothing in that report. Please correct it. It is unfair for both the parties."

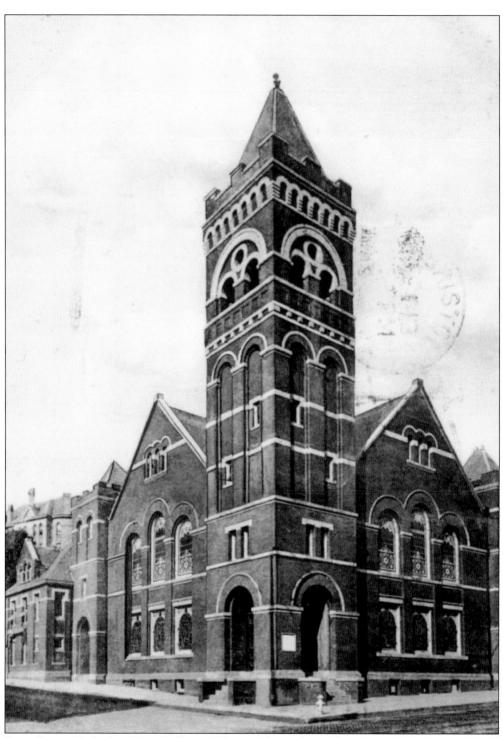

State Street Methodist Church, Bristol, Tenn. A beautiful edifice of mixed Romanesque and Gothic elements, the State Street Methodist Church solidly occupies a downtown corner. The card was mailed in 1907; there was no message.

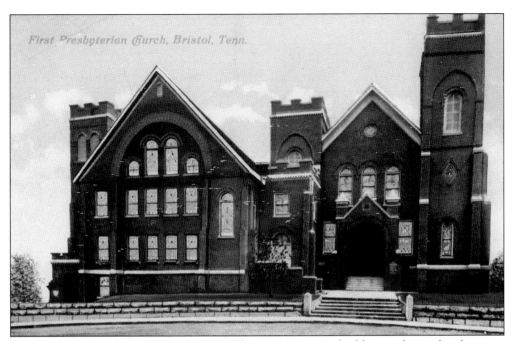

First Presbyterian Church, Bristol, Tenn. The compact main building and crenelated towers, along with the numerous windows, give this church a unique appearance.

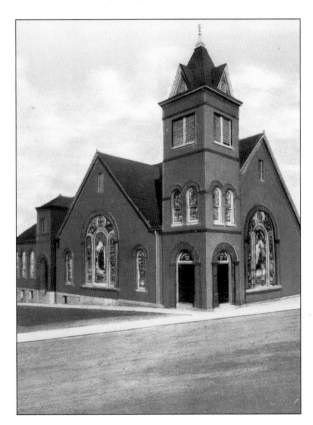

Central Christian Church, Bristol, Tenn. A small edifice with a single tower and two large, elaborate stained glass windows, the Central Christian Church sits at the corner of Sixth and Broad Streets.

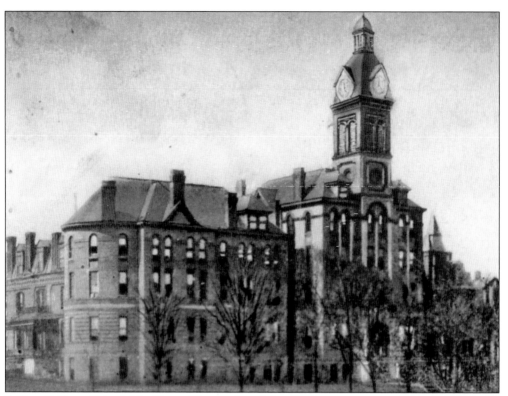

Sullins College, Bristol, Va.-Tenn. The sender of this 1909 picture postcard wrote: "Hello old boy—I have had a good time and fixing to start back Monday. I sure hate to leave the children."

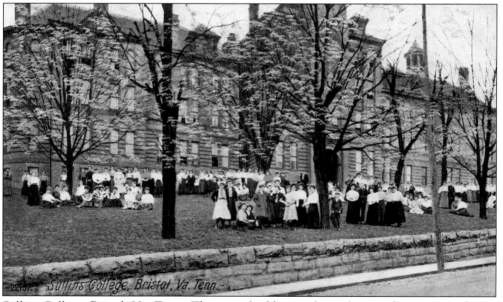

Sullins College, Bristol, Va.-Tenn. The main building is shown here without its cupola top and clock tower. Among all the girls on the lawn one small boy may be seen. Sent in 1909, the card's message informs: "Reached here on time from Bristol. Hope you both stood the trip well." It was mailed from Johnson City.

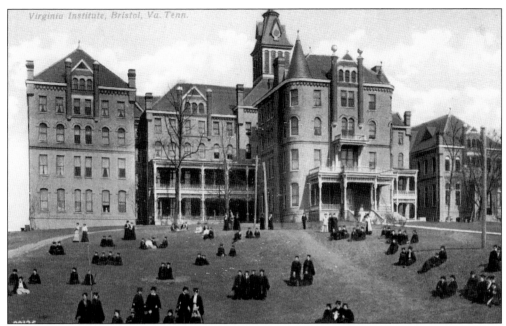

Virginia Institute, Bristol, Va.-Tenn. We see here another prestigious school for girls which opened in 1907. This card, dated April 12, 1909, reads: "Am working hard every day will be in Jonesboro Sunday hope your cold is better will be in Knox soon how did you enjoy the play."

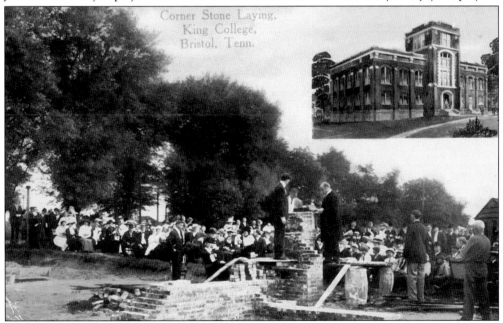

Corner Stone Laying, King College, Bristol, Tenn. This card shows the laying of the cornerstone of the Alumni and Old Students Building at King College by the General Assembly of the Southern Presbyterian Church on May 22, 1912. The assembly was present, as were distinguished alumni of King College, including Dr. R.D. Reed of Columbia, who presided; Dr. J.I. Vance of Nashville, who delivered the address; and Dr. Clyce, moderator of the assembly, who is shown with trowel in hand in the act of placing the cornerstone.

19

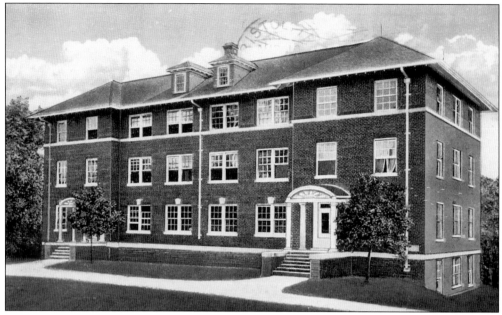

King College, New Dormitory, Bristol, Tenn. The new dormitory was built in an unadorned, practical style, with no attempt to emulate past decorative motifs. The card was mailed in 1929, and its sender merely writes: "Brother Billie."

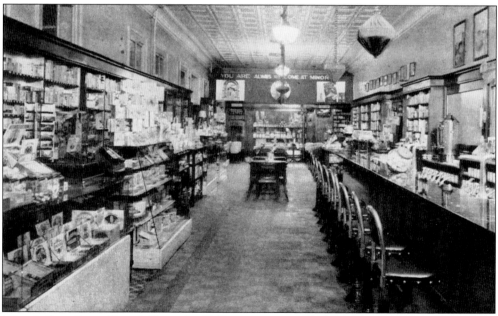

Minor's Drug Store, Bristol, Tenn. In 1940 a customer could have his prescriptions filled; buy sick room supplies, cigars, and cosmetics; and enjoy the delights of a soda fountain, all in one store. The sender of the card writes hurriedly: "Just got married. See you Tues."

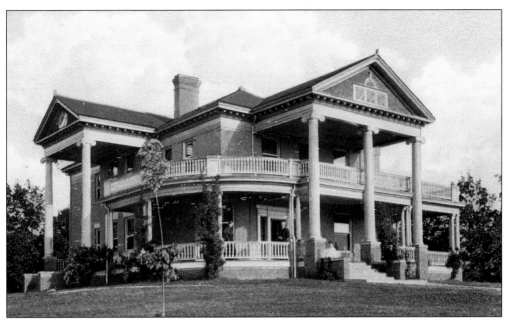

J.M. Barber's Residence, Bristol, Tenn. This beautiful Greek Revival home, with its portico and wide verandas, is typical of the homes built around the turn of the century by wealthy families. Looking closely, one can see Mr. and Mrs. Barber on the lower veranda, and a young boy sitting on the stoop.

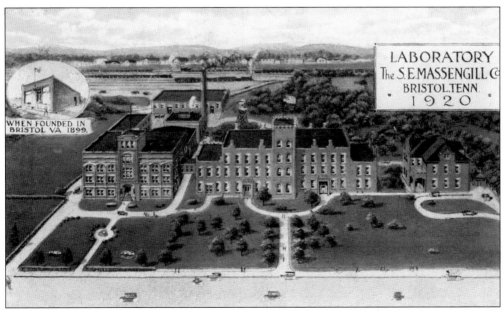

LABORATORY
The S.E. MASSENGILL Cᵒ
BRISTOL, TENN.
• 1 9 2 0 •

WHEN FOUNDED IN
BRISTOL VA. 1899.

Laboratory, the S.E. Massengill Co., Bristol, Tenn This advertising card shows the progress of a large company from its founding in 1899 to the date of the card, 1920.

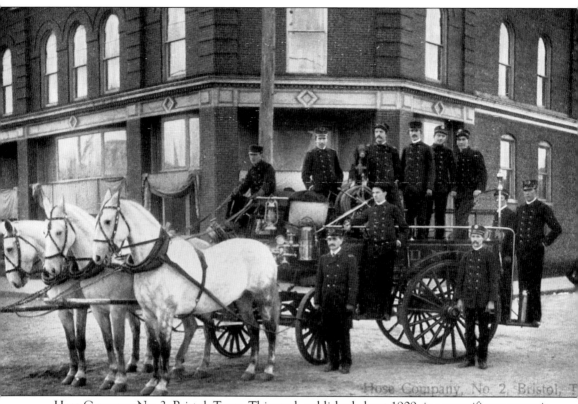

Hose Company No. 2, Bristol, Tenn. This card, published about 1909, is a magnificent portrait of the fire equipment and the men who operated it. The horses, too, are majestic, and the urchin in the street is full of admiration.

Two

ELIZABETHTON
Carter County

Elizabethton is almost as old as Tennessee; it was laid out and designated the Carter County seat in 1797. Located at the foot of Lynn Mountain, east of the Doe River, it was first known as Watauga Old Fields, then named Elizabethton for Elizabeth Maclin Carter, the wife of Col. Landon Carter, for whom the county was named.

Duffield Academy was established in 1806 and continued well into the next century. The historical marker for the academy, located on Academy Street, is made of stones taken from the foundation of the academy.

Some of the early factories in Elizabethton were the Watauga Woolen Mills, Bradley Lumber Company, Jenkins Flour Mill, and Dixie Chewing Gum Factory. In 1926 a group of German industrialists started the first spinning machine of the American Bemberg Corporation which preceded the North American Rayon Corporation here.

In 1839 Parson Brownlow published his *Elizabethton Whig*. *The Elizabethton Republican and Manufacturers Advocate* was published until 1844 when fire destroyed its offices. Recovery from the Civil War was very slow, not really beginning until the 1890s.

The oldest covered bridge in Tennessee crosses the Doe River in Elizabethton. Built in 1882 at a cost of $3,000, it has been called "Queen of the South," and "The Kissing Bridge." It is the most photographed and the most admired historical structure in Carter County, and it is one of the few covered bridges in the South that is still in use. With a span of 134 feet, the bridge was praised at the time of its construction as an engineering feat, and it is listed in the *Historic Engineering Record*. It withstood the great flood of 1901 which destroyed all other bridges along the Doe River.

One of Elizabethton's most impressive historic sites, John and Landon Carter house (known as "The Mansion") was built in or about 1780. A two-story structure of the Georgian Colonial type, with large stone chimneys at either end and wide hand-hewn clapboards over logs, it is one of the oldest buildings remaining in Tennessee, and possibly the only remaining link to the Watauga Association. The hall and some rooms are beautifully paneled and the high windows contained the first glass panes on the frontier. Many heirlooms remain in the house. The Alfred Moore Carter home on Elk Avenue, one of the finest Federal-style structures in Tennessee, was constructed in 1819. It is a plain two-story structure covered with tongued-and-grooved, hand-hewn, hand-planed boards. It features large, double-hinged windows. It is a handsome example of complex, over-delicate, late Federal style. The mantelpieces are especially noteworthy. Alfred Moore Carter was the son of Landon C. Carter. Alfred's son, Samuel P. Carter, who was born in this house, became a brigadier general during the

Civil War, and later an admiral in the navy. He is the only man in United States history to achieve both ranks.

Robert L. Taylor (1850–1912) and his brother Alfred A. Taylor (1848–1931), governors of Tennessee, were born and reared in Elizabethton. Bob Taylor was a lifelong Democrat, Alf an ardent Republican. As young men in 1886 they campaigned as opposing candidates for the governorship of Tennessee. Bob was elected and served three terms, from 1887 to 1891 (two terms) and from 1897 to 1899. He later became a senator. Alf was governor from 1921 to 1923.

The Elizabethton area has seen a number of events that can truly be said to have shaped American history. The Sycamore Shoals Monument on Highway 321 near the city is a three-sided shaft of river rocks erected to mark the site of Fort Watauga and the events that took place there. The first permanent American settlement outside of the original thirteen colonies was established here, and in 1772 the Watauga Association, the first majority rule system of American democratic government, was formed.

The Transylvania Purchase, the largest real estate transaction in United States history, took place on March 17, 1775, at Sycamore Shoals. The Transylvania Company, led by Richard Henderson of North Carolina, purchased over 20 million acres from the Cherokees for 2,000 pounds sterling and goods worth 8,000 pounds. Fort Watauga, built nearby, became a refuge for settlers in 1776 when the Indians, aided by the English, besieged the fort. The pioneers did not surrender, and the Indians departed.

The Battle of King's Mountain resulted from a plan formed at the September 25, 1780, assembly of Overmountain Men. About 1,100 fighting men marched over the mountains in search of British Major Patrick Ferguson and his Tory militia. On October 7, 1780, the Overmountain Men, led by John Sevier and Isaac Shelby, found Ferguson's army at King's Mountain, South Carolina, and in little more than an hour had defeated them. This victory has been described as a crucial first link in a chain of events that led to the eventual surrender of the British forces in the Revolutionary War. In Elizabethton, the Soldiers' Monument on the court house lawn bears an inscription honoring Mary Patton, who made the gunpowder fired by the Tennesseans at the Battle of King's Mountain. A boulder monument marks the spot where the Watauga Association was organized in 1772.

Between Elizabethton and Johnson City we find the Sinking Creek Baptist Church. Built in 1803, the log building is the oldest Baptist church in Tennessee. The congregation was established in the 1770s when a preaching revival took place in the home of Charles Robertson in Sinking Creek. In 1924 the original church was restored and enlarged. Sunday school rooms were added in 1940, and in 1962 a new church was built near the old one. The Sinking Creek Baptist Church Historical Society has now restored the log building and it has been enshrined as a special property of the Wataugua Association of the Baptist Church.

About 20 miles southeast of Elizabethton on Highway 143 is Roan Mountain, one of the highest peaks (6,313 feet) in the United States. On the side of the mountain is a 600-acre rhododendron garden, one of the largest in the country. Visitors can enjoy the area at the Roan Mountain State Park.

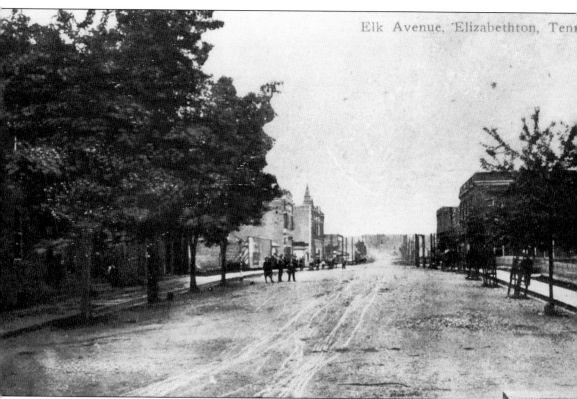

Elk Avenue, Elizabethton, Tenn. This 1911 postcard shows a time before main streets were paved, or even graveled, and life was a little slower. The sender is laconic: "Regards to all. Ernie."

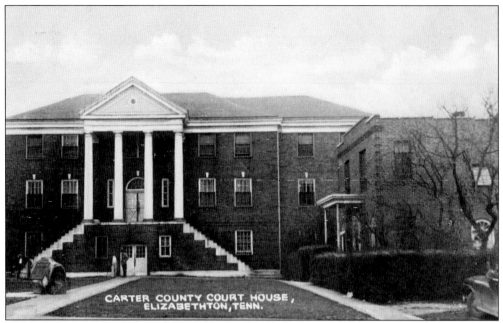

Carter County Court House, Elizabethton, Tenn. Constructed during the 1850s, the Carter County Court House has been altered several times. On the grounds there is a boulder with a plaque commemorating the Watauga Old Fields, where the Watauga Association was formed.

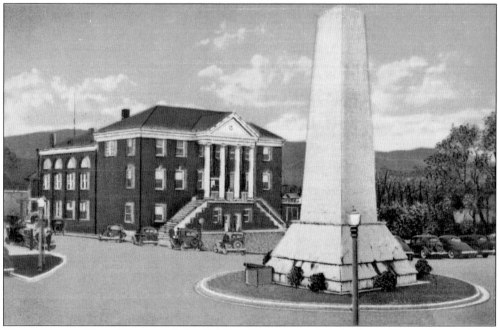

Carter County Court House and the Soldiers Monument, Elizabethton, Tenn. The Soldiers Monument is a 65-foot shaft of cement built as a memorial to all soldiers who fought between 1776 and 1912, when the monument was dedicated.

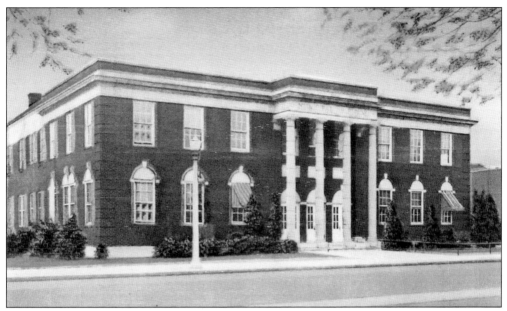

Municipal Building, Elizabethton, Tenn. This building has the familiar public edifice look of a red brick box with pseudo-Greek columns added in front. The custodian evidently forgot to align the awnings before the picture was made.

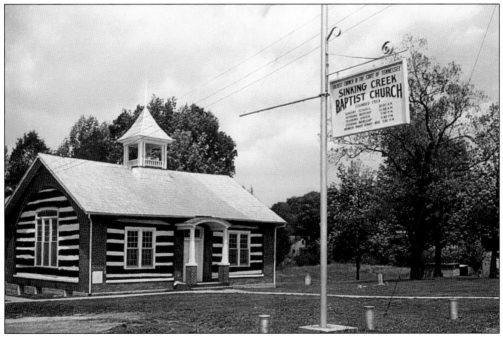

Sinking Creek Baptist Church, near Elizabethton, Tenn. Located "down the road" from Elizabethton on the way to Johnson City, Sinking Creek Baptist Church is the oldest church in Tennessee. It was founded in 1783.

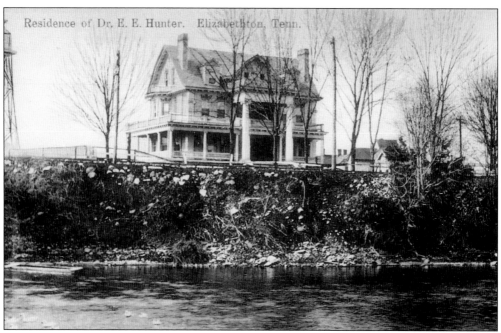

The Residence of Dr. E.E. Hunter, Elizabethton, Tenn. An imposing house high on the river bank, this combination of Federal and Greek Revival architecture was common at the turn of the century.

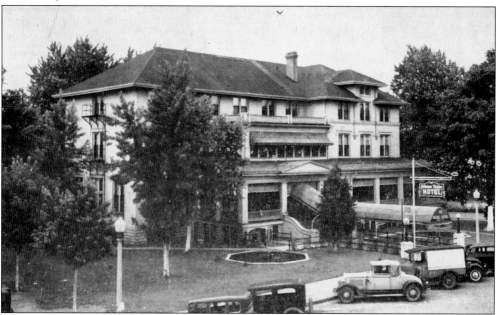

The Governor Taylor Hotel, Elizabethton, Tenn. This postcard can be dated from the printed information on the back: "Located in a beautiful mountain setting beside a rippling stream; accepted by a year-round clientele of traveling men desiring comfort and economy; enjoying a seasonal tourist patronage; privileged to continue to serve Rotary, Kiwanis, other civic organizations, and the leading families of Elizabethton and their visiting friends. Rates: Rooms, $1. to $3.50. Meals, 35¢, 65¢, and 75¢."

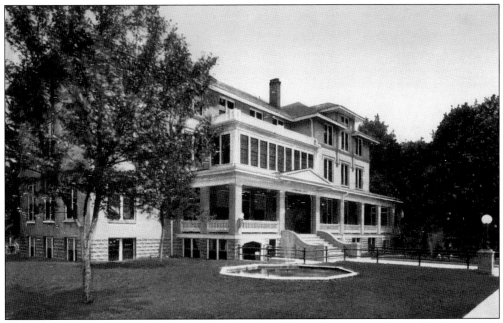

The Lynnwood Hotel, Elizabethton, Tenn. Looking like a large tourist home, the Lynnwood Hotel has an inviting appearance enhanced by a comfortable veranda. In the days before air conditioning came into use, a veranda was a prized adjunct to a building.

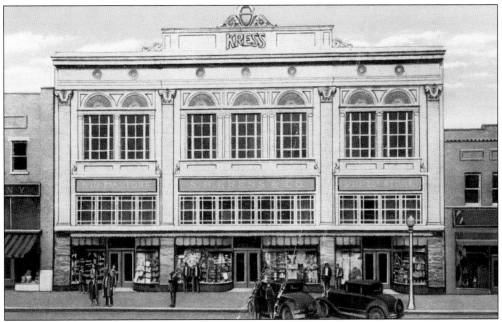

S.H. Kress and Co., Elizabethton, Tenn. This mammoth "5 and 10" took up three storefronts in the 1930s. The automobiles appear to be 1932 models.

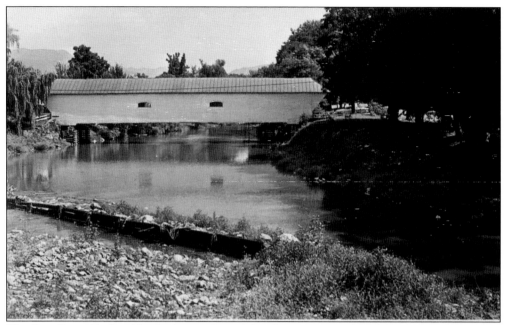

The Doe River Bridge, Elizabethton, Tenn. This famous covered bridge over the Doe River at Elizabethton was constructed of massive oak pieces held together with steel spikes. Heavy weatherboarding was placed over a vertical wood structure topped by a heavy overhanging roof. In spite of necessary renovations from time to time, the bridge's handbuilt craftsmanship has not been basically altered.

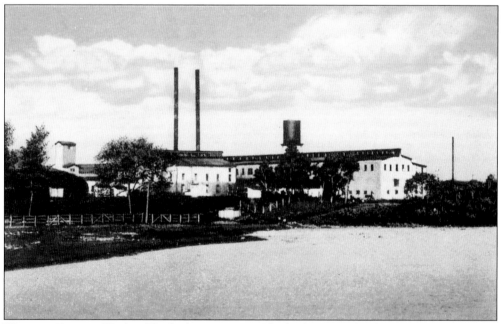

Watauga Extract Works, Elizabethton, Tenn. Elizabethton is the home of several large manufacturing plants. The Watauga River, which flows by the city, is the origin of the name.

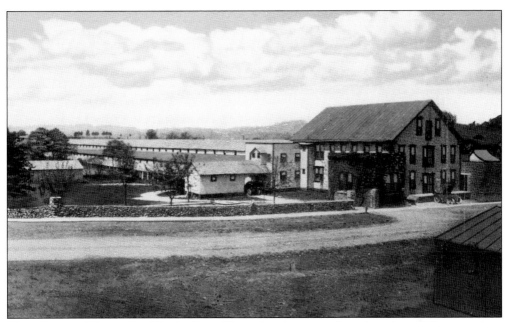

Tenn. Line and Twine Co., Elizabethton, Tenn Another manufacturing plant with tremendous output is the Tenn. Line and Twine Co., demonstrating the versatility of manufacturing in this area.

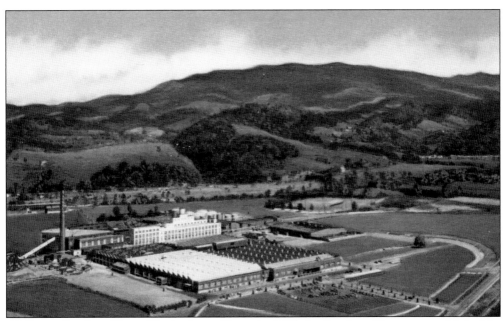

American Bemberg Plant, Elizabethton, Tenn. In 1926 the Bemberg Plant was established by a group of German industrialists. "Bemberg" came to mean more than just a giant artificial silk producing plant; on Fifth Avenue in New York it meant the cloth of evening dresses.

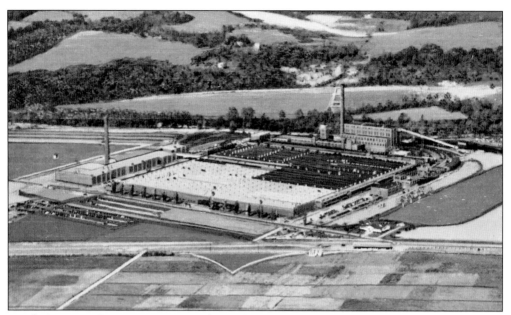

North American Rayon Corporation Plant, Elizabethton, Tenn. Another large manufacturer of "artificial silk" is located in Elizabethton.

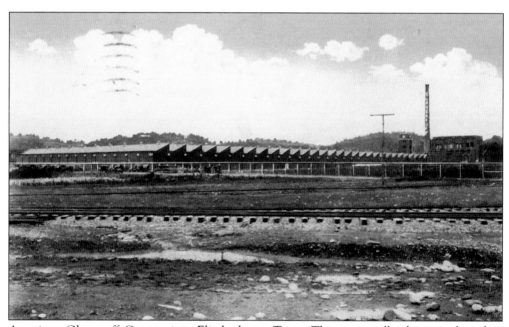

American Glanzstoff Corporation, Elizabethton, Tenn. This rayon silk plant employs four thousand people and represents an investment of $50 million. It located in Elizabethton in 1927.

Three

JOHNSON CITY
Washington County

The Johnson City area was settled in the 1770s by pioneers who were part of the Watauga Association in 1772 and the State of Franklin in the 1780s. The first settler was David Jobe, who came in 1777. Development of the region progressed slowly until 1854, when Henry Johnson arrived from North Carolina and opened a store. At that time the settlement was known as Blue Plum, but it has changed names a number of times since those early days. After the East Tennessee & Virginia Railroad (now part of the Southern Railroad) built a water tank here in 1858, Johnson built a depot at his own expense, and trains were scheduled to stop at the community that then became known as Johnson's Tank or Johnson's Depot. During the Civil War the town was called Haynesville in honor of Landon Carter Haynes, who was greatly responsible for bringing the railroad through northeastern Tennessee.

After the war Henry Johnson resumed his activities as postmaster, depot agent, merchant, hotel keeper, and magistrate. When the city was granted a charter of incorporation in 1869, Johnson was elected its first mayor, and the town was named Johnson City.

Railroads made Johnson City the principal city in Washington County. The first large industry was a tannery, established in 1882; the next year saw the Johnson City Foundry and Machine Works and the Carnegie Furnace Company set up.

The first school appeared in 1864 and in 1867 Science Hill Male and Female Institute was founded (it later became Science Hill School). East Tennessee State Normal School opened in 1911, its goal being to improve teacher training in the state. At first offering a two-year teacher-training degree, it expanded the program to a three-year one in 1919, and further expanded it to a four-year course in 1924. In 1930 the name of the school was changed to East Tennessee Teachers College. Located at the western end of West Maple Street, in 1939 it had a 140-acre campus, 90 acres of which were covered with woods and farmland. The eight buildings of modified Georgian design were constructed of red brick with limestone trim. After another name change in 1943 to East Tennessee State College, the college was finally named East Tennessee State University in 1963. It now covers 366 acres and offers classes in seventy major fields of study and forty masters programs.

Johnson City began to grow rapidly after the establishment of the rayon plants to the east in Elizabethton. Large numbers of people could not find living quarters in the boom city and so came to live in Johnson City.

On Lamont Street one finds the entrance to the United States Soldiers Home. The home really is a city-within-a-city: it has its own post office, its own fire and police departments, its own waterworks, and a telephone system. There are 448 acres of landscaped grounds and the 57 buildings are constructed of brick and stone in modified Italian Renaissance style. The institution accommodates 3,500 patients and has an average of 400 hospital cases and 2,000 permanently disabled residents. Handicraft training is given to the residents who sell their products to visitors. All the paper poppies sold annually by Veterans of Foreign Wars are made here. The Soldiers Home was established in 1903 through the efforts of Congressman Walter Brownlow for the care of aged Union soldiers. It was used for the care of tubercular ex-service men after World War I, and then later converted to its present use.

The Tipton-Haynes Historic Site, located on Buffalo Road, is one of Tennessee's treasures. The original home was built in 1784 by Col. John Tipton (1730–1813), considered to be one of the founding fathers of Tennessee: he signed the Constitution of Tennessee and served as a delegate to both the United States and the State of Franklin's Constitutional Conventions. The estate is the site of the Battle of the Lost State of Franklin. John Tipton, Jr., inherited the home in 1813, and in 1839 the estate was given as a wedding present to Landon Carter Haynes (1816–1875), who enlarged and renovated the mansion. Haynes was a member of the state legislature, speaker of the house, a presidential elector in three elections (1844, 1848, and 1860), and the person for whom Haynesville (later Johnson City) was named.

Route 36 becomes South Roan Street, where we find Robin's Roost. Built in 1890, the building was bought and named by Bob Taylor in 1892. It was purchased in 1900 by Alf Taylor, who lived here until 1903.

Milligan College, a private, co-educational, and non-sectarian institution, was established in 1881 by Joseph Hopwood, a Kentuckian, on the site of Buffalo Institute, which had been opened before the Civil War. The name was changed in 1882 to Milligan College to honor Robert Milligan of Kentucky University, one of Joseph Hopwood's teachers. Today the four-year college of arts and sciences is affiliated with the Christian Colleges and Churches of Christ. Milligan offers BS and BA degrees in fifteen fields of study, as well as a Master of Education program. The campus spans 145 acres, and has 22 buildings and an average annual enrollment of 800 students.

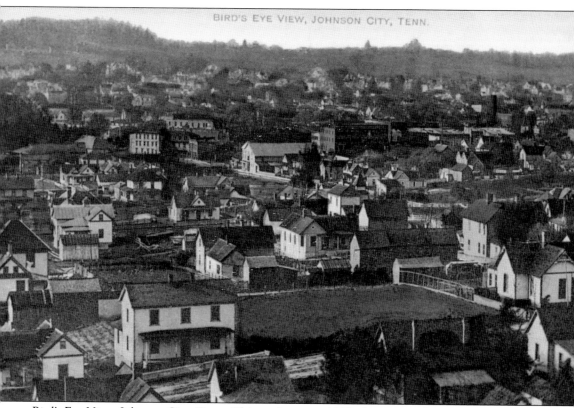

Bird's Eye View, Johnson City, Tenn. This card, sent in 1908, shows a residential area of frame houses in the plain Colonial style. The sender says that she "Arrived safe Mrs. V. met me here, all want to be remembered to you all look after my Tim until I come back."

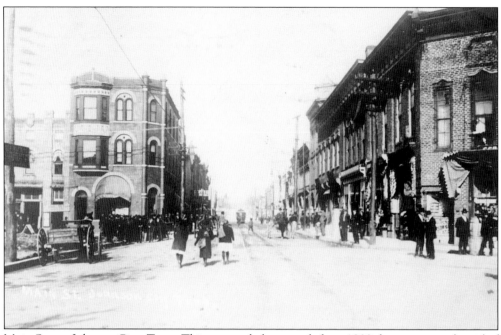

Main Street, Johnson City, Tenn. This postcard photograph from 1909 shows a street devoid of vehicles (except for a distant trolley) but filled with pedestrians. The sender writes: "I arrived this morning all ok. Go to work tomorrow. Have been awful lonely since Wednesday night. Let me hear from you soon."

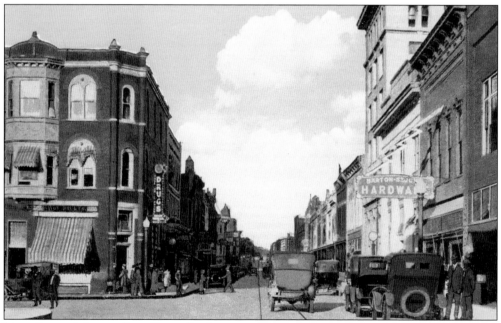

Main Street, Johnson City, Tenn. By the time this card was made around 1920, Main Street was bustling with automobiles; commercial signs had made their appearance; and one building had added a story.

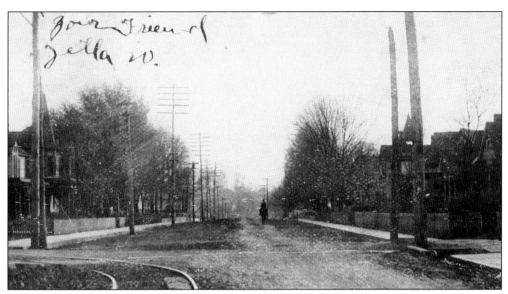

Watanga (sic) Avenue looking West, Johnson City, Tenn. This 1909 card shows a dirt street and part of a trolley track. The street name is misspelled; it should read "Watauga Ave." A rather sloppy message was attempted on the front of the card; only the name and address of the recipient was allowed on the back. The message reads: "Dear Lida, I received your postal the other day. I can walk on my foot now. I live Elizabethton now. I like this place fine but I want to see Ralph Robert and Lucie. My address will just be Elizabethton, Tenn. I got a card from Edith the day you left our home. Your friend, Zella W."

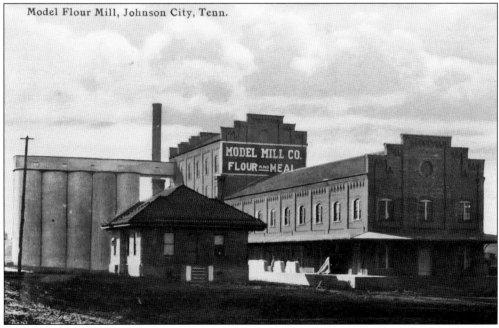

Model Flour Mill, Johnson City, Tenn. According to the advertisements, the daily capacity of this mill was 500 barrels of flour, 2,500 bushels of meal, and 50,000 pounds of feed. In 1913 this card carried the message: "I am here. Everything looks the same as it did before I left hope everything is all right there." (Postcard courtesy of Paul Garland.)

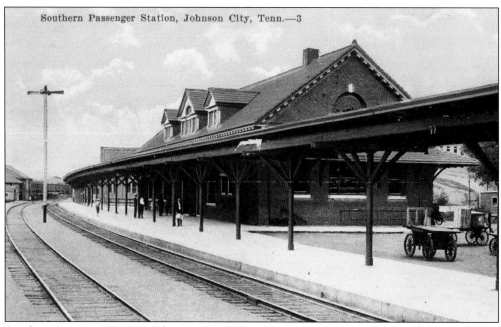

Southern Passenger Station, Johnson City, Tenn.—3

Southern Passenger Station, Johnson City, Tenn. The coming of the railroad to Johnson City in 1908/09 made the city an industrial center. A key railroad junction, Johnson City was the hub of shipments in and out of factories which located here. A resident capitalist was Clinchfield Railroad's George L. Carter.

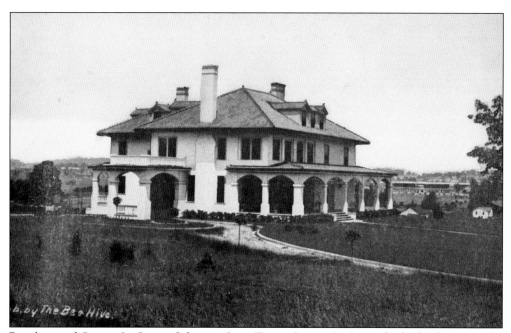

Residence of George L. Carter, Johnson City, Tenn. George L. Carter built this home in the southside neighborhood in 1909. He was an investor in local industry and real estate, including the land on which East Tennessee Normal School was constructed.

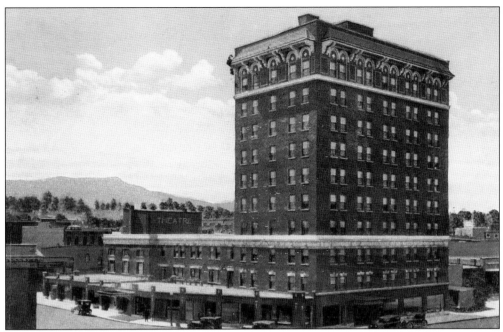

The John Sevier Hotel, Johnson City, Tenn. In 1927 this large hotel had a temporary resident who sent this card to Pittsburgh: "Dearest Betty, Thank you for the Easter telegram it came as we were going to breakfast and it was very kind of you to send it. We are on our way to Hot Springs!"

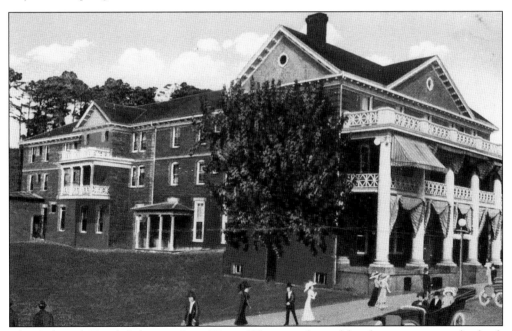

The Colonial Hotel, Johnson City, Tenn. We are informed by the printing on the back of the card that "Colonial Hotel, Inc. has been in operation for more than 50 years and is noted for comfort and hospitality—in the heart of the business district but away from the noise of the railroad." .

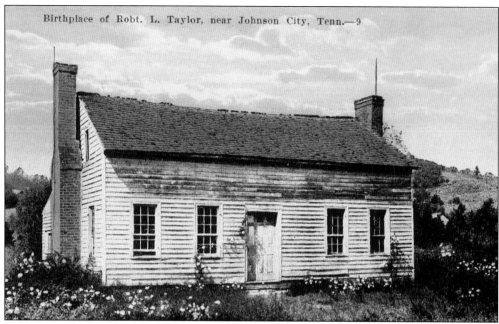

Birthplace of Robert L. Taylor near Johnson City, Tenn. Robert L. Taylor is one of the famous political Taylor brothers who were governors of Tennessee. The birthplace is usually given as Elizabethton, but the house is between the two cities and each claims the distinction.

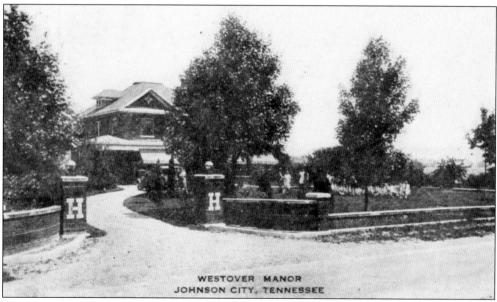

WESTOVER MANOR
JOHNSON CITY, TENNESSEE

Westover Manor, Johnson City, Tenn. This 1937 advertising card says that Westover Manor is famous from coast to coast for delicious home-cooked meals. The sender is on a trip of some dimension: "Dear folks, Washington 8 a.m. Skyline Drive. Lexington 1 p.m. Bristol, Tenn., and now here. Cold as heck! Snow falling on the peaks."

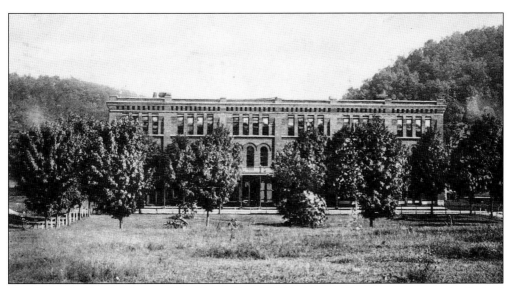

The Carnegie Hotel, Johnson City, Tenn. Dated 1907, this card has its message on the limited white space on the front: "Doesnt this look nice? We were out there yesterday. It is just as pretty as this looks."

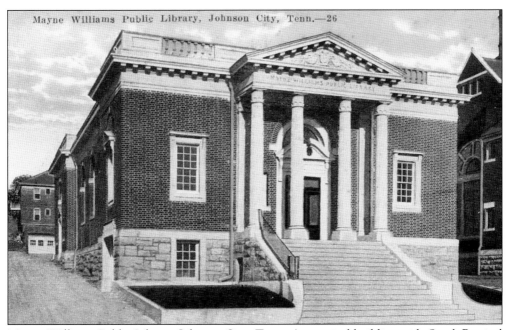

Mayne Williams Public Library, Johnson City, Tenn.—26

Mayne Williams Public Library, Johnson City, Tenn. A practical building with Greek Revival columns and pediment, the public library combines elegance and useful modernity. One wonders whether everyone could manage those seventeen steps.

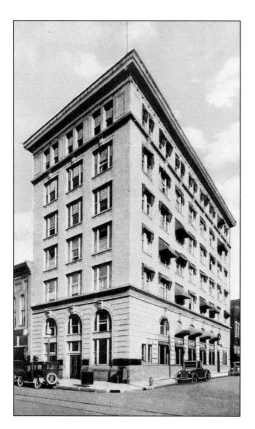

Hamilton National Bank Building, Johnson City, Tenn. Many public buildings of this period, especially banks, tend to look like up-ended boxes. Skyscrapers were on the rise. The first elevator was installed in a public building in 1871; thereafter, one had to look up.

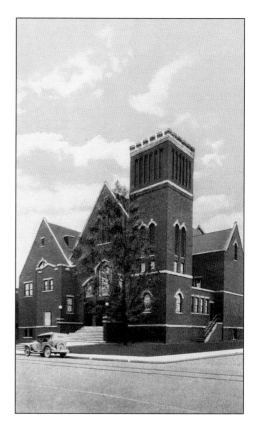

First Presbyterian Church, Johnson City, Tenn. Many Presbyterian churches of the early decades of the twentieth century have a compact look, with square, crenelated towers. The church pictured here on a 1920s postcard is a good example.

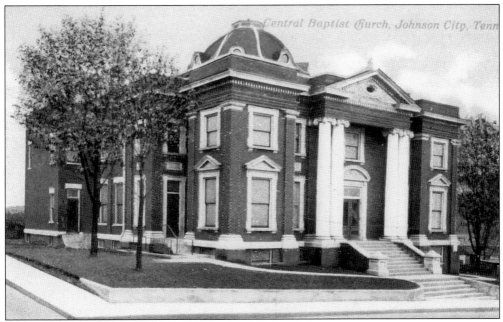

Central Baptist Church, Johnson City, Tenn. Greek Revival influences front the building., but a hint of Queen Anne permeates the brick work and the roof. The sender of this card (undated) merely writes: "From your friend Calvin."

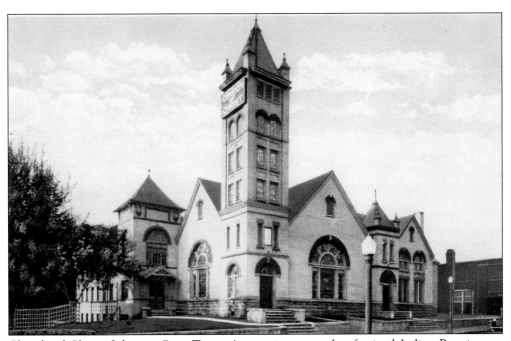

Church of Christ, Johnson City, Tenn. A stunning example of mixed Italian Renaissance Revival elements, the church features peaked roofs and towers and large stained glass windows. It was dedicated in 1906. The sender says: "Sorry I haven't had time to write. I wired Jack money last night. He is on his way home. Oh, boy am I excited."

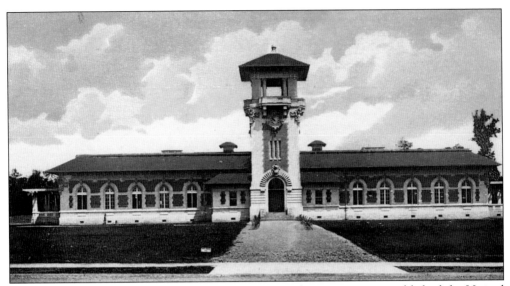

Mess Hall, N.H.D.V.S., Johnson City, Tenn. In 1903 the government established the United States Soldiers Home, a retirement and medical facility for former Union soldiers. There are 36 buildings in the complex covering 447 acres. The architecture, Renaissance Revival, is outstanding. The sender of the card writes this: "This is the dineing room hall whire 1200 goes to eat and all eat at one time. The anechels (sic) on the other side stands fore these words. N is fore national—and H is fore home and D is fore disabled—V is for volentered-S is for soldiers."

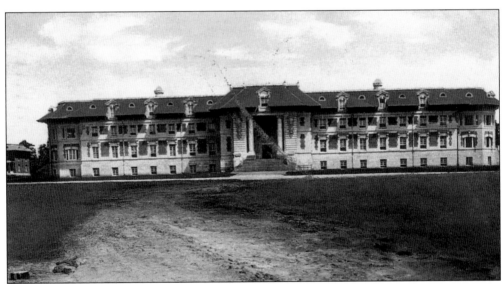

Barracks 1 and 2, N.H.D.V.S., Johnson City, Tenn. The N.H.D.V.S. became a branch of the Veterans Administration in 1930. The complex is also called Mountain Home. This card, sent by a patient in 1908, reads: "I wonder if you have not entirely forgotten that there is such a creature as I. How is life serving you? I should think you would at least send a fellow a postal for old times sake if nothing else. I do hate to be forgotten as I am, and by my best cousin, too."

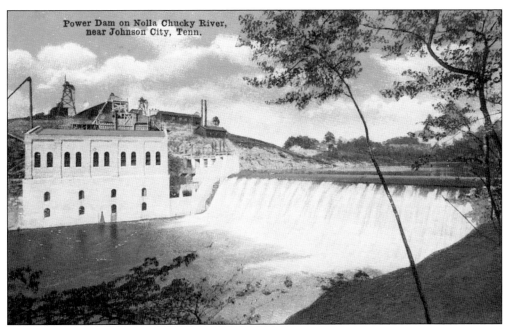

Power Dam on Nolla Chucky River near Johnson City, Tenn. Power is generated here for industrial and domestic purposes in the Johnson City area. This card, sent in 1920, reads: "Your letter at hand—will write soon. Busy last week cleaning house and canning 2 bu. pears."

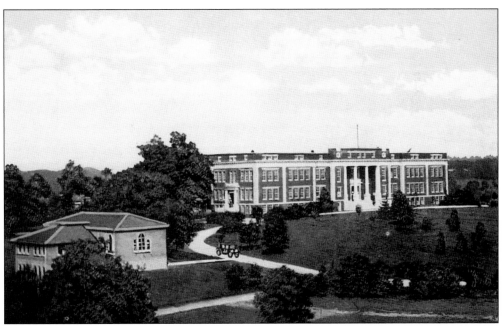

View of the Campus of East Tennessee State Normal School, Johnson City, Tenn. This teacher-training college opened in 1911. The first name change—to East Tennessee Teachers College—occurred in 1930. The name would change twice more before becoming East Tennessee State University.

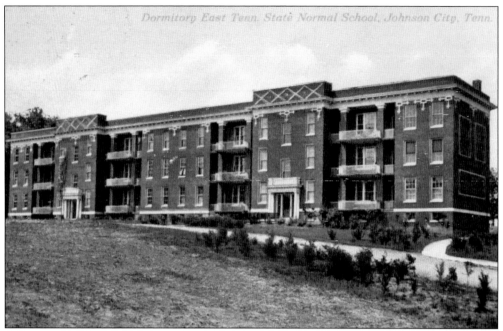

A Dormitory at East Tennessee State Normal School, Tenn. The correspondent, mailing this card in 1913, had little to say: "In Johnson City. To Birmingham Saturday am. Feeling fair. Best wishes. Rush card. Train here."

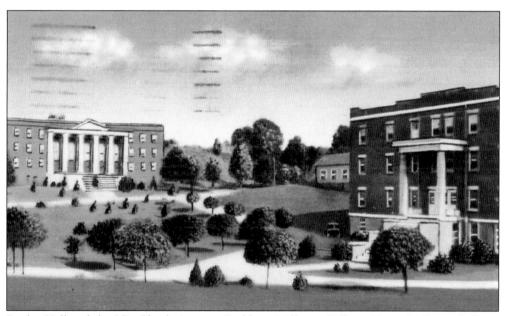

Pardee Hall and the J.D. Cheek Activity Building, Milligan College, Tenn. Milligan College, founded in 1882, is situated between Elizabethton and Johnson City. It is nondenominational, but "the Bible is central to a curriculum that unites humanities, sciences, and fine arts into a Christian world view."

Four

JONESBORO
Washington County

Jonesboro, located 6 miles west of Johnson City and actually named "Jonesborough" since 1983, is the oldest town in Tennessee. It was established in 1779, seventeen years before North Carolina became a state, by the North Carolina Assembly. The town was named for Willie Jones (1740–1801), a North Carolina politician who was influential in helping Tennessee break away from North Carolina and Virginia. It became the county seat of Washington County, a political sub-division of North Carolina and the first county in the United States to be named for George Washington.

As the seat of government, the new town grew; and when in 1784 North Carolina ceded its western lands to the federal government., the people formed a state of their own—the State of Franklin—complete with governor, legislature, courts, and militia. Jonesboro was its first capital and legislative sessions were held here until 1785, when the seat of government was moved to Greeneville.

From the first there was a town plan and building codes, so Jonesboro became the first planned community in the United States west of the mountains. No ramshackle cabins were permitted; the owner of each lot had to build "one brick, stone, or well-framed house" and failure to comply meant forfeiture of the land. Residents remain very proud of their picturesque town with its variety of architectural styles, which range from neoclassical to Victorian.

Andrew Jackson established his law practice here in 1788. Jonesboro was also the home of William and Matthew Atkinson, who designed the great seal of the State of Tennessee in 1801.

In 1840 a spot on Main Street was the scene of a memorable encounter between William G. (Parson) Brownlow and Landon Carter Haynes. Brownlow had printed some unkind statements about Haynes in his newspaper, *The Whig*, and in response Haynes denounced Brownlow publicly. They fought it out, Brownlow receiving a bullet in his thigh and Haynes a severe beating around his head. Haynes later became a member of the Confederate Congress, and Brownlow became governor of Tennessee (1865–67).

The famous Chester Inn, or Jonesboro Inn, on the corner of Main and Cherokee (the former Great Stage Route from Washington) was built in 1798 by William P. Chester. It was for many years the oldest frame structure in town. Three presidents of the United States—Jackson, Polk, and Johnson—have been entertained here, and many other notable people, including Charles Dickens, have stopped here. The building is only one of several architecturally significant stage inns built here. A first floor room was for a time the office of Brownlow's *Whig*.

The courthouse, in the center of town, was designed by Baumann and Baumann in 1912. First built in 1779, it has subsequently been rebuilt five times. The two-story brick structure is surmounted by a central clock tower in two stages, the first of which is columned. A balustraded parapet surrounds the roof, and each of three fronts has a pedimented portico. On the northeast corner of the courthouse lawn there is a Boone Trail marker in the shape of an arrowhead.

The First Presbyterian Church, at 206 W. Main Street, was dedicated on August 15, 1850. Resting on a high basement with a panelled entrance, the structure was built in Greek Revival style. Above the simple pediment rises a Victorian steeple with pinnacles on the four corners of the first stage. It has a slave gallery and retains the original pews and pulpit.

The 1845 Methodist Episcopal Church South, at 215 W. Main Street, is a one-story brick, Greek Revival structure with an Ionic portico, having four columns and an unusual window in the pediment. A steeple with three stages surrounds the edifice.

The first paper established in America to advocate the abolition of slavery, Elihu Embree's *Manumission Intelligencer*, was first printed in 1815 at the office of *The East Tennessee Patriot* in Jonesboro. Embree's own *Emancipator* followed, beginning publication in 1820.

There are at least twenty-seven other historic sites and notable buildings to see in Jonesboro. Among them are the 1852 First Baptist Church; the 1847 United Methodist Church, housing a notable bell in the steeple; and Sister's Row, a block of three townhouses built in 1820. Jonesboro in its totality is one of Tennessee's treasures.

Eight miles south of Jonesboro near Telford is Washington College, which began as Martin Academy in 1777 and is credited as the first institution of learning west of the Alleghenies. In 1778, Reverend Samuel Doak came as teacher; in 1795 the institution was incorporated as Washington College. Doak, a Pennsylvania Presbyterian and Princeton graduate, brought the first books into Tennessee on the back of his horse while he himself walked. A pioneer educator and staunch searcher for right and truth, his is a unique history in the annals of Tennessee education. In 1818 he left Washington College to join his son in a new collegiate endeavor which ultimately became Tusculum College.

For many years Washington College was the foremost college of classical learning on the western frontier. It was nearly destroyed in the Civil War, but around 1900 it was functioning well and had established a self-help program for mountain students. In 1920 a high school was added; in 1923 the college curriculum was terminated; and in 1939 the building was being used as a county high school. Seventh and eighth grades were added in 1978, and today the co-educational boarding and day school enrolls students in grades five through twelve. A college preparatory institution, it is now named Washington Academy.

The Salem Presbyterian Church, on the campus of Washington College, was one of four churches founded by Samuel Doak in and around 1780, and is therefore one of the three oldest Presbyterian congregations in the state still in use. The present structure was begun in 1895, and much of the construction work was done by students and faculty, who molded and fired the brick. The rose window in the church is one of only three of its kind in the United States. The names of the Doak men can be found in the memorial stained glass windows. Samuel Doak is buried on the campus; the school and surroundings became his greatest memorial.

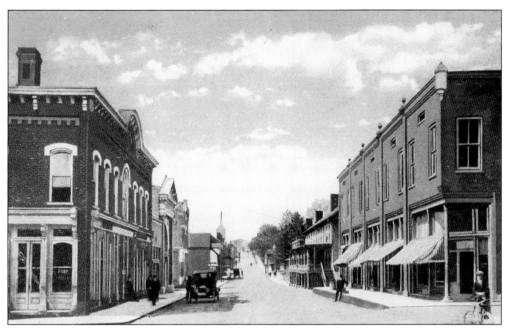

Main Street looking West from the Post Office, Jonesboro, Tenn. A postcard mailed July 24, 1920, shows Jonesboro's quiet Main Street in midsummer. The sender writes: "We are having a good visit here with my sister. I hope Miss Effie is o.k. by now. We will leave here Monday for Troutville and hope to get to Timberville Thurs. Suppose you are at council today."

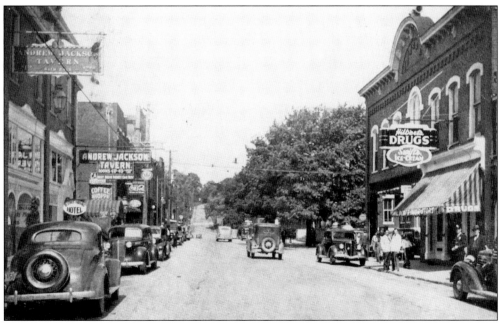

Main Street looking East, Jonesboro, Tenn. Twenty years later, Main Street has changed: one notices automobiles and signs in particular.

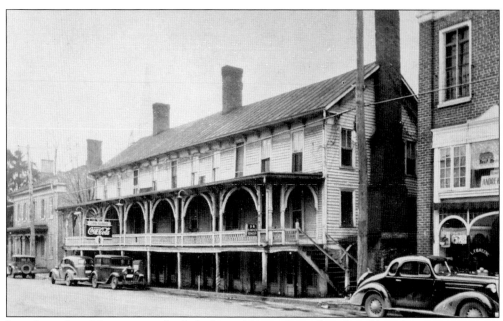

Jonesboro Inn. The inn was built before 1800, making this the oldest frame structure in town. Andrew Jackson held a reception here in 1832. The cars in the picture date this scene to the 1930s.

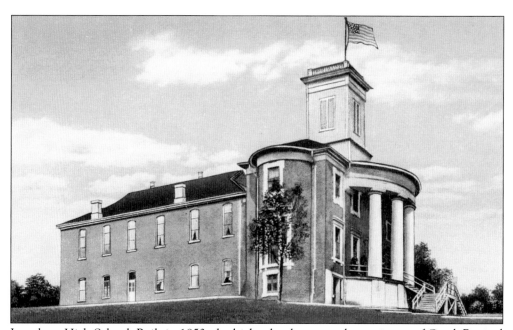

Jonesboro High School. Built in 1853, the high school seems to be a mixture of Greek Revival and Renaissance elements. There is an incongruity between the solidity of the structure and the makeshift appearance of the front steps.

Washington County Court House, Jonesboro, Tenn. Built in 1912 by the architects Baumann and Baumann, the court house is constructed of brick and topped by a two-tiered clock tower. Many other elegant additions were used: there are three fronts, each with a pedimented portico, and a parapet with balustrade surrounds the roof. The correspondent who mailed this card in 1914 is irritated: "I was glad to get your card. I didn't know you could write. I sent cards to Stuart and Garland. They were tickled to get them."

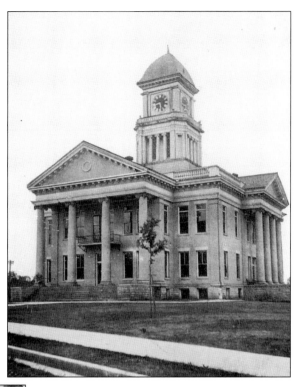

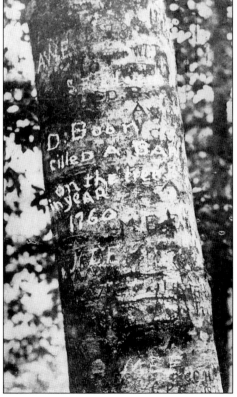

The Historic Daniel Boon Tree near Jonesboro, Tenn. This beech tree, no longer extant, was located 7 miles north of Jonesboro. It bore a knife-carved inscription: "D Boon cilled a Bar on the Tree in year 1760." This postcard was mailed in 1907, the sender writing the message on the border: "Dear F, Your letter came yesterday. Will answer soon. We are moving to Chatt. Tenn. I am very sorry about the horse for I know how you feel. Love to all. B."

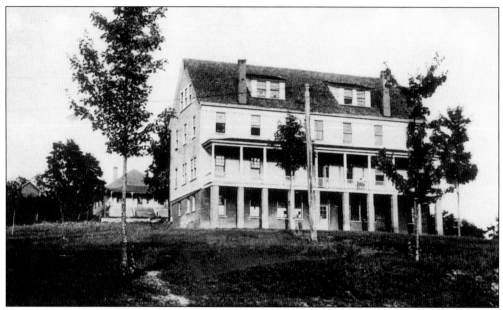

Boys' Dormitory at Washington College, Tennessee. In 1783 Reverend Samuel Doak organized a log school near Jonesboro which he called Martin's Academy. This was the first school west of the Appalachians. In 1793 the academy became Washington College. In 1920 a high school was added, and in 1923 the college curriculum dropped. This card is undated, but it would seem to have been made prior to 1923.

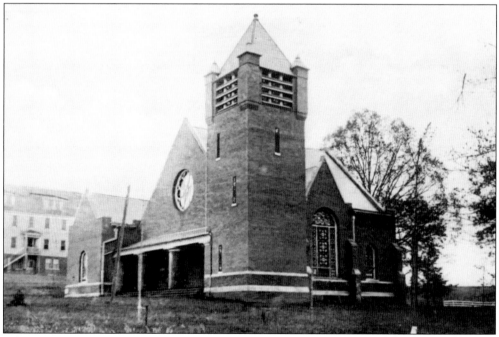

Salem Church at Washington College, Tennessee. Located on the campus of Washington College, Salem Presbyterian Church, founded by Samuel Doak, is home to one of the three oldest Presbyterian congregations in the state.

Five

ERWIN
Unicoi County

Erwin lies 14 miles south of Johnson City on Highway 19-11E in the valley between the Unicoi, Buffalo, and Rich mountain ranges. In the eighteenth and nineteenth centuries hunters camped here and dressed their kills, and the settlement was known as Greasy Cove. For a while in the 1890s residents wanted to name the town "Vanderbilt" for George Vanderbilt who was looking for a site to build his mansion. When he went to Asheville to build, the name "Erwin" was chosen, probably in honor of Jessie B. Erwin, the first county clerk.

The town's destiny was tied to the railroad. By 1899 Unicoi County had a rail line from one end to the other—the Carolina, Clinchfield, & Ohio (CC&O). The CC&O cost $30 million, and was it was called "the costliest railroad in America" by the *Scientific American Supplement*. In 1909 CC&O located its repair shops at Erwin; the general offices were established here in 1926.

The most picturesque part of the railroad runs from Unaka Springs through the Nolichucky Canyon. This railroad winds its way, snake-like, for 20 miles through chasms, gorges, ravines, and cliffs which extend up thousands of feet. In places the gorge is only 250 feet wide and the tracks are built on the sides of the cliffs. Today a special train is run in the fall so that tourists can view the foliage along this beautiful route.

The railroad also played an important role in a strange event which brought Erwin a great deal of publicity. On September 12, 1916, a circus elephant named Mary, who weighed 5 tons and was larger than the famed Jumbo, killed her handler during a parade in Kingsport. It was decided that she should be executed, and several methods were tried: she was shot, to no avail; she was electrocuted (44,000 volts), with no results. It was then suggested that she should be taken to Erwin, placed on the tracks, and crushed between two locomotives. In the end, however, it was decided that she should be hanged. She was transported to Erwin amid much publicity, and after much difficulty she was hanged from a crane at the railroad yard as five thousand spectators watched. The event was featured in Ripley's Believe It or Not on August 29, 1938.

Along Ohio Avenue in Erwin are company homes for workers in the Southern Potteries. They came in 1917 from Ohio and West Virginia where the American pottery industry was centered; the railroad donated the land and built forty homes here. Charles W. Foreman, one of the owners, experimented with a hand-painting process in imitation of Ming china, applying metallic-based colors, then glazing. He perfected the process at Erwin and the result was "Blue Ridge Hand Painted under the Glaze" dinnerware. It enjoyed national publicity and became world famous. There were more than fourteen thousand patterns originated by native artists. The pottery boom in Erwin ended about 1957.

A marker in Erwin calls attention to the old Greasy Cove Race Track, the scene of a race between one of Andrew Jackson's horses and one owned by Col. Robert Love of Jonesboro. Jackson challenged Love to a race but when he was defeated he lost his temper and quarrelled with Love, who called Jackson "a long, gangling, sorrel-topped soap-stick." Friends had to intervene to prevent a fight.

Erwin is noted for its fish hatchery dating from 1897: the United States Fish and Wildlife Service's oldest hatchery. It hatches thirteen million trout eggs each year. At first the distribution of fish was by rail; later when roads became better, trucks were used. The water source is a natural spring that supplies 1,200 gallons of water per minute. Nearby is the road to Unaka Springs, a resort popular for its iron and sulphur waters.

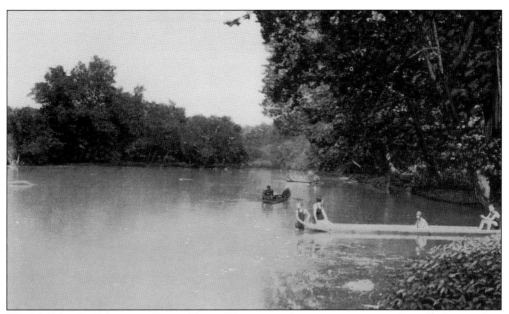

The Nolichucky River near Erwin, Tenn. This river, whose name is variously spelled, meanders through the Nolichucky Gorge amid scenery of majestic splendor. Nolichucky comes from the Cherokee word Nula-tsu-gu-y, which has been interpreted to mean "rushing water."

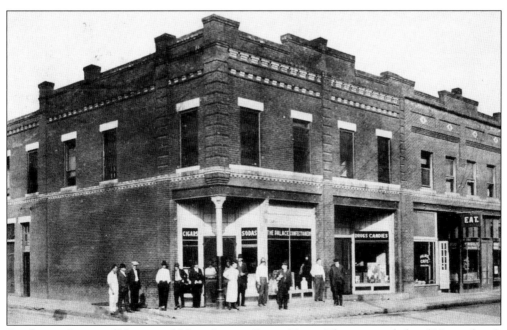

Southwest Corner of Union and Main Streets, Erwin, Tenn. This postcard, dated November 6, 1925, reveals a "busy" corner in a small town. A confectionery store is on the corner; a waiter wearing his apron is one of the people pictured. A cafe adjoins, whose sign is brief and to the point, saying only "EAT."

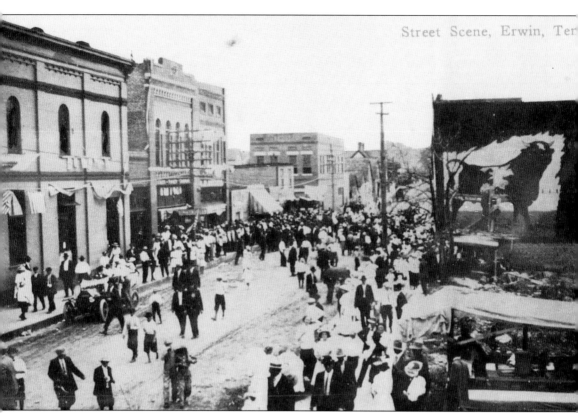

Street Scene, Erwin, Tenn. The scene here may be one of some celebration, but it is hard to tell. Many men are wearing knickers; the women's dresses indicate that the time is around 1910. There is no date, but the sender says, "Dear Nell, Do you know this place?... it is the great city of Erwin. Hope you are having a fine time."

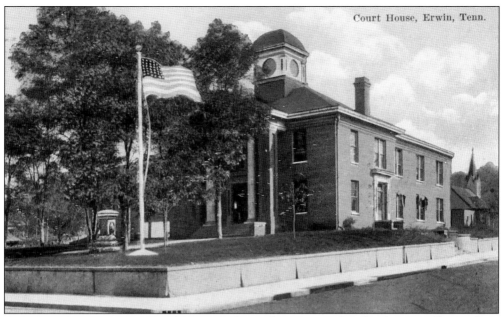

Court House, Erwin, Tenn. On this postcard a mother writes to her daughter: "Hello, Bertha. I guess you thought I fell in and couldn't get out but I have bin so lazy since I came here how are you all Ethols sister had an offle reck in a car none serious hurt but bad enough, geting along as well as can be expected. Mother."

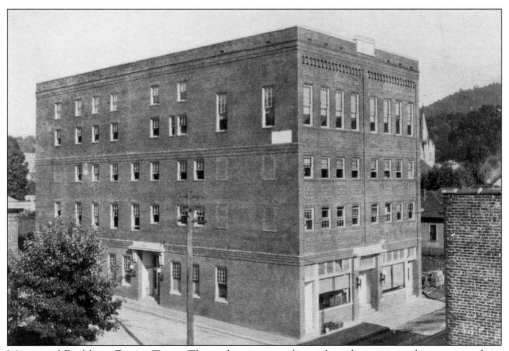

Municipal Building, Erwin, Tenn. The utilitarian rectilinear box design is used once more for a public building. No effort is made to stylize the effect; however, the numerous small rectangular windows give it a style of its own.

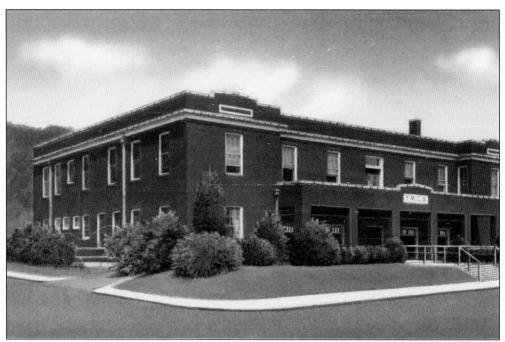

YMCA Building, Erwin, Tenn. Another brick box, with some finesse on the front, is the YMCA. It reflects the design of the 1920s and 1930s.

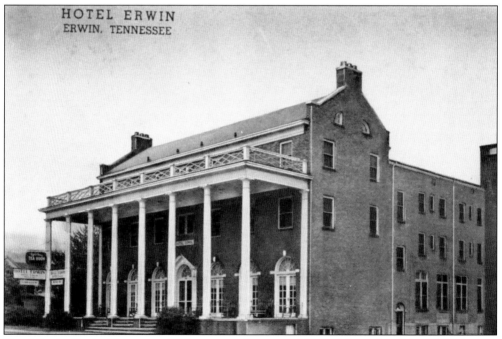

Hotel Erwin, Erwin, Tennessee. This structure has genteel Colonial touches. Mrs. C.S. Morgan, manager, promises that the hotel is: "Modern- Comfortable-'Our Home Your Home'-Home of the Famous Rainbow Tea Room." It is "air conditioned" and has "home-cooked foods." It is located on U.S. Highway 19 and 23.

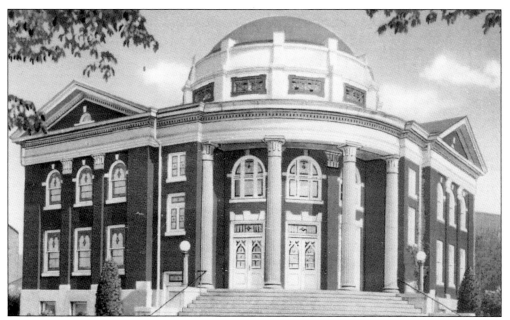

Erwin Presbyterian Church. A church of some size, judging from the card, featuring Greek Revival columns and pediments, the Erwin Presbyterian is replete with many windows and an impressive dome.

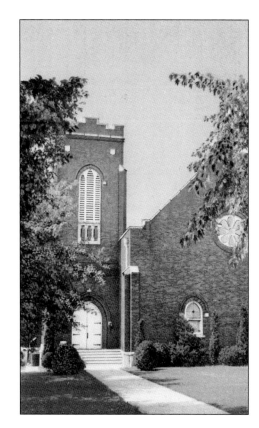

Centenary Methodist Church, Erwin, Tenn. A heavy Romanesque look with a hint of Gothic in the slightly pointed windows is the sum of Centenary. It combines compactness and delicacy.

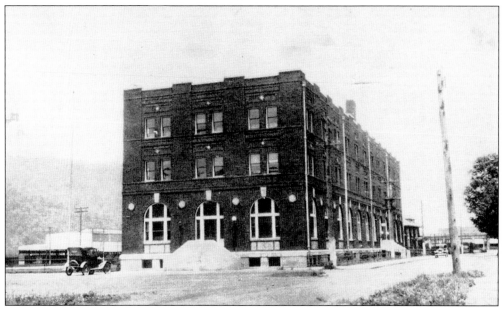

CC&O Office Building, Erwin, Tenn. CC&0 stands for Carolina, Clinchfield, and Ohio. Adjacent to the Clinchfield Depot, this office facility is one of several support buildings needed at a large railroad yard. This picture was made in the 1920s.

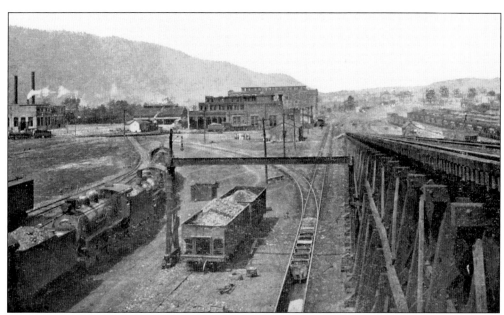

CC&O Railway Shops, Erwin, Tenn. Erwin has become the last of the major Clinchfield Railroad towns in Tennessee. The railroad profoundly influenced the life of the city from its beginnings.

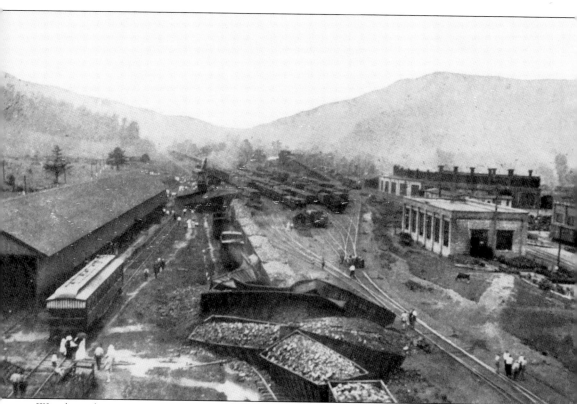

Wreck on the CC&O Railroad on July 18, 1919, near Erwin, Tenn. Once in a while a catastrophe becomes the subject of a postcard picture. With a date it becomes part of history.

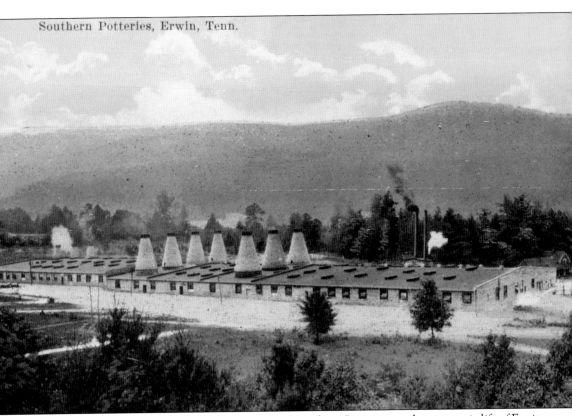

Southern Potteries, Erwin, Tenn.

Southern Potteries, Erwin, Tenn. The impact of Southern Potteries on the economic life of Erwin was very great between 1917 and 1957. Its Blue Ridge dinnerware became world famous.

Six

TUSCULUM
Greene County

Proceeding southward on US 11E, through Limestone and Afton, we pass through Tusculum and note the college there. Established in 1818 by Samuel Doak and his son Samuel Witherspoon Doak, it was named Tusculum after the home of President John Witherspoon of Princeton University, where the elder Doak had been a student. When the elder Doak died in 1829, school operations were suspended, but in 1835 his son reopened the school with four students. By 1840 the number had grown to seventy students. In 1868 the school merged with Greeneville College (founded in 1794 by Reverend Hezekiah Balch) and became present-day Tusculum, which has the distinction of being the second-oldest school of higher learning west of the Appalachians.

All the buildings are of brick and stone except for one wooden structure that was built in 1825: the Samuel Doak House. Eight buildings were erected between 1841 and 1928, the oldest of these being Old College, built in 1841 by slaves whom Samuel Witherspoon Doak then freed upon completion of the project. McCormick Hall, named in honor of Cyrus McCormick of International Harvester fame, was built in 1887. Craig Hall, built in 1891, was the result of money given by Mrs. Nettie Fowler McCormick, who named it in honor of her pastor. Mrs. McCormick's generosity also provided for Virginia Hall, built in 1901. This building was named for her daughter and designed by the famous Louis A. Sullivan; it is one of only three buildings in the South that he designed.

Tusculum was the twenty-eighth college founded in America. It is the oldest college in Tennessee and the oldest co-educational college associated with the Presbyterian Church. The Andrew Johnson Library and Museum is the state's largest presidential library; it houses almost two hundred original Civil War-era newspapers from cities throughout the country.

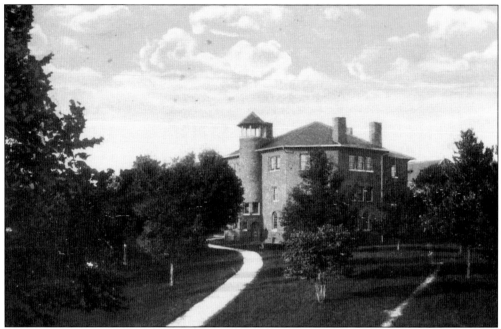

McCormick Hall, Tusculum College. This card, mailed in 1922, reads: "Dear Gladys, Sorry I haven't a birthday card for you, but I can't get any around here. However, my wishes for your birthday are just as sincere written on this card as on a real birthday one. I hope you get all the gifts you want and more beside."

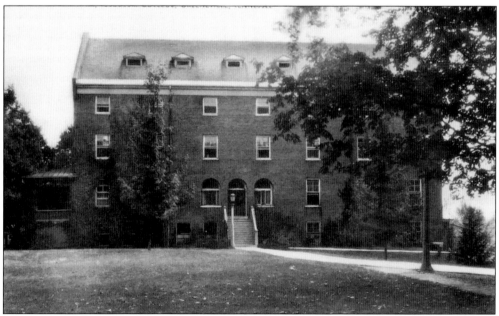

Virginia Hall, Tusculum College. Mrs. Nettie Fowler McCormick gave the money to build Virginia Hall and named it in honor of her daughter. It was designed by Louis A. Sullivan, whose work in Southern states is limited to this, and only two other buildings.

Seven

GREENEVILLE
Greene County

Both Greene County and the town of Greeneville were named for Nathaniel Greene, the Revolutionary War general. The county was formed in 1783 when Washington County was partitioned and Greeneville was chosen as county seat. Greeneville was also the capital of the ill-fated State of Franklin during its last two years (1785–87).

The first schools were taught in a log house and the in Presbyterian church. Rhea Academy opened in 1812 and additions were made in 1825 and 1840.

Andrew Johnson (1808–1875) moved to Greeneville from North Carolina at the age of seventeen, and within a few weeks opened his tailor shop. In 1827 he married Eliza McCardle, who taught him to write. He entered local politics in Greeneville and in 1829 was elected alderman. In 1843 he went to Congress, serving there until 1853. He then served as governor of Tennessee (1853–57) and as military governor of Tennessee (1862–65). He was inaugurated Vice-President of the United States on March 14, 1865, and succeeded Lincoln as President after the latter's assassination in April 1865. His career in Washington as president was difficult and controversial; he missed impeachment by only one vote in the senate.

After his presidential term, Johnson returned to his Greeneville home, the Andrew Johnson Home on West Main Street, which was completed in 1851. It is a two-and-a-half-story brick structure with a many-gabled roof and a long one-story porch, and it stands flush with the sloping street. The parlor furnishings of Johnson's time have been preserved.

The Andrew Johnson Tailor Shop, on the corner of Depot and College Streets behind the county court house, is a small frame structure now enclosed in a brick building. Over the door is the sign proclaiming "A. Johnson, Tailor."

On a hill at the corner of Main and College Streets is the court house, its lawn exhibiting many historic markers. The site of the capitol of the State of Franklin is commemorated by a bronze tablet in the wall at the front entrance to the court house. The Morgan Monument, commemorating the death of General John H. Morgan, the Confederate Terrible Raider who was killed here, is located on the court house lawn. The lawn is a favorite gathering place, and on Saturdays farm families flock to Greeneville, which is primarily a farmers' trading center.

The First Presbyterian Church, designed by Coile and Cardwell, stands on Main Street one block north of the court house. Erected in 1912, it was built to a modified Greek Revival design. Resting on a high basement, the balustraded portico is approached by a wide central stair. Four Doric columns support a simple pediment which is surmounted by a steeple in three stages. The walls and columns date from 1848.

To the west along Main Street are fine old houses; towards the east is the business section; and to the south stretch stockyards, creameries, poultry houses, coal yards, and the warehouses in which millions of dollars worth of tobacco are sold annually.

Two notable houses are: Boxwood Manor at 209 Brown's Hill, an ornately trimmed brick house dating from 1855; and the Sevier-O'Keefe House, the home of Valentine Sevier, brother of John Sevier, and probably the oldest house in town.

The Dickson-Williams House is a particularly outstanding building. The mansion, of Federal design, was built in 1825 by the county's first postmaster, William Dickson, as a wedding gift to his daughter Catherine. Within, there is a circular staircase which rises three full flights. Occupying a whole block, the home covers a site now bounded by Main, Church, Irish, and Depot Streets, and is surrounded by gardens. Many celebrities—Presidents Johnson and Polk, and Marquis de Lafayette among them— were entertained here.

St. James Episcopal Church, built around 1850, was designed by George M. Spencer. It is a combination of Greek Revival and Italianate architecture, with pointed windows and Gothic details. It has an exceptional interior, with walnut woodwork and pews, a slave gallery, and the oldest working organ in the state.

The Asbury United Methodist Church was completed on April 12, 1912. The name Asbury dates back to Bishop Asbury, who was a guest in Greeneville in 1790. The architectural design is predominantly Greek Revival, and the structure contains a number of outstanding stained glass windows.

After the Civil War Greeneville increased in population and wealth. Manufacturing and the tobacco trade were the leading industries. Among many notable businesses at this time were East Tennessee Manufacturing Company, Greeneville Manufacturing Company, Brown and Mosier (handles and spokes), Lamon Brothers (wagons), Spencer and Brown (drugs and medicines), Stephen Brothers (woolens), and R. Snapp and J.R. Brown (tanneries).

The Andrew Johnson National Cemetery lies on a hill, at the top of which is an Italian marble monument marking President Johnson's and Eliza's graves. The monument was erected by the Johnsons' surviving children and dedicated in 1878. It is 27 feet tall, and features an eagle on top of a globe. An inscription reads: "His faith in the people never wavered." President Johnson was the first person to be buried here; he was joined later by his family and veterans of all subsequent wars.

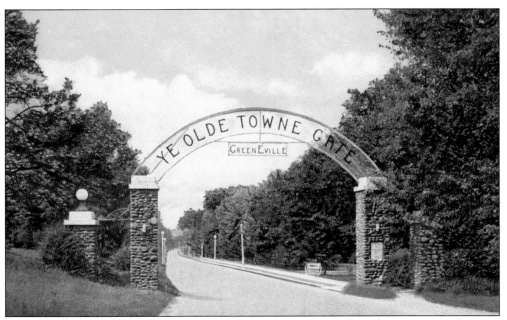

Ye Olde Towne Gate, Greeneville, Tenn. Greeneville was established in 1783 and for more than two hundred years it has been a regional agricultural center. It is also the region's largest tobacco market. In 1926 the local garden club built this entrance gate to welcome visitors to the city.

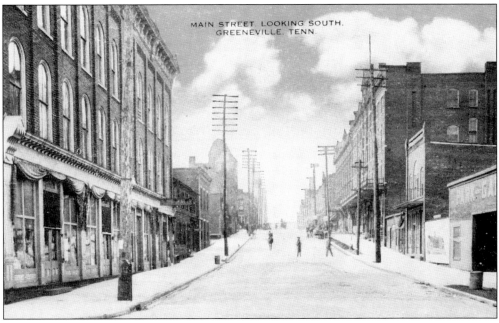

Main Street looking South, Greeneville, Tenn. This early postcard shows an almost deserted downtown street, with only two wagons to be seen in the distance. The stores look rather unkempt. The four-story Hotel Brumley, in the right foreground, was built at 109 North Main Street in 1884.

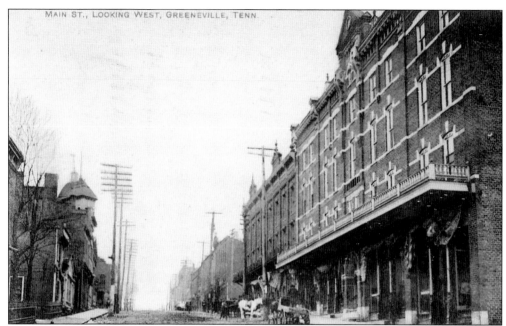

Main Street looking West, Greeneville, Tenn. When this photograph was taken the street was still being used by wagons and horses. This card was mailed on March 17, 1910. The correspondent writes: "I just landed in house from my real home was on the Atlantic and sure had one more time. My boss paid my salary all the time I was gone."

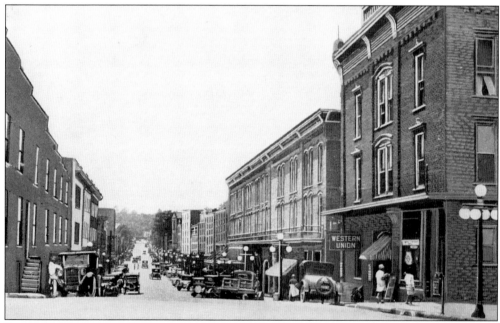

Depot Street, Greeneville, Tenn. Automobiles have invaded the town by about 1930. Depot Street, of course, was the location of the Southern Railway Passenger Station, not shown in the picture.

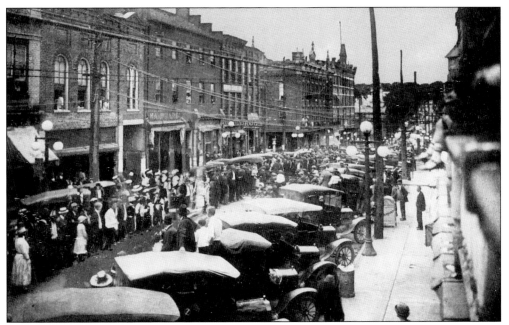

Main Street looking North, Greeneville, Tenn. The masses of people on the street suggest that a parade or celebration may have been taking place on the day this photograph was taken, though it is not visible in this shot. The number of cars made parking a real problem even then. The designs that can be seen indicate that this image dates from the early 1920s.

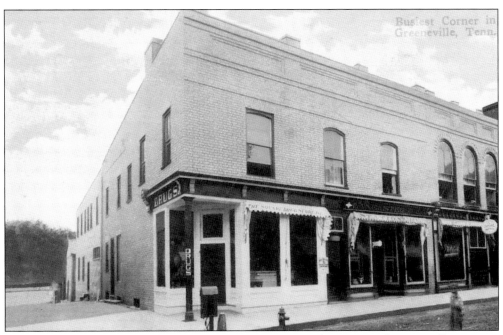

Busiest Corner in Greeneville, Tenn. For some reason, the picture does not illustrate its title. A joke from the photographer, perhaps? We see the usual—the Square Drug Store, Inc., and Lancaster's Stationery Store. The street is unpaved, and there seems to be a boy in the foreground.

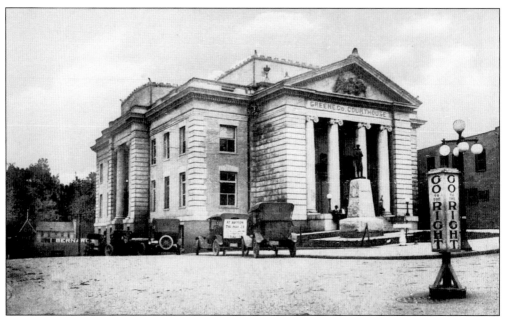

Greene County Court House, Greeneville, Tenn. Located at the corner of Depot and Main Streets, the court house sits on a small hill overlooking Main Street. Its lawn exhibits many historic markers; a bronze tablet commemorating the site of the Capitol of the State of Franklin may be found at the front entrance. The court house was built in 1916.

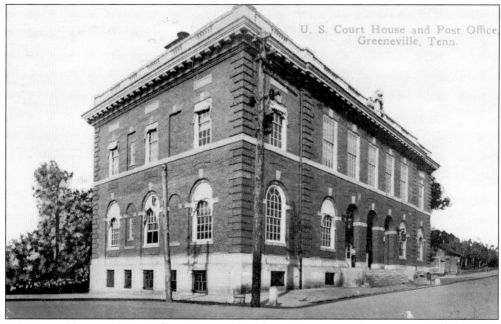

U.S. Court House and Post Office, Greeneville, Tenn. This postcard was sent to Oklahoma in 1915, and reads: "Hello, John, how are you? Hope you are fine and dandy and not melting like I am. Hope to write a letter soon. I have not forgotten you."

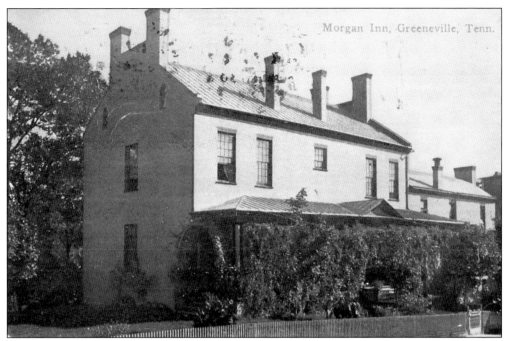

Morgan Inn, Greeneville, Tenn. This card was sent to Ohio in 1915. The sender writes: "My dear Grace, You are certainly a dear to be so thoughtful of me. Lovely weather. Housecleaning next week. Last school lecture Wed. eve. The 'Singin Skule' given by the Baptist Ch. was fine—so funny—home talent. So you will soon be home. Then I will see you."

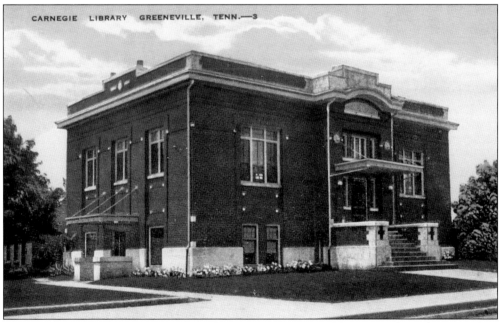

Carnegie Library, Greeneville, Tenn. This Carnegie Library, like most others, has a modest, utilitarian appearance. The benefactor, Andrew Carnegie, gave over $43 million in his lifetime to build numerous such libraries all over the country.

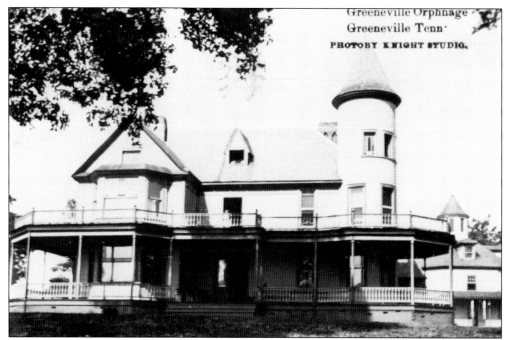

Greeneville Orphnage
Greeneville Tenn·
PHOTO BY KNIGHT STUDIO.

Greeneville Orphanage. This spacious Victorian structure was pictured on a card in 1908. The sender writes: "Seeing your request for post cards, I send one from the 'Sunny South.' Many a little tot is made happy and comfortable at the home here pictured."

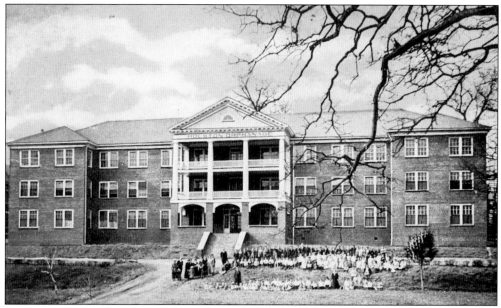

Wiley Memorial Building at the Holston Orphanage, Greeneville, Tenn. This card was mailed in 1930, and the sender wrote, apparently on behalf of a young charge: "We want to thank you very kindly indeed for the Easter box so kindly to Gertrude. It made her very happy indeed to be remembered at this time. Yours sincerely, J. L. Hardin, Supt."

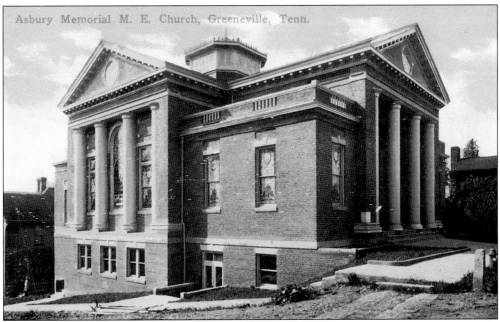

Asbury Memorial M. E. Church, Greeneville, Tenn.

Asbury Memorial M.E. Church, Greeneville, Tenn. Dating from 1912, Asbury M.E. Church memorializes Bishop Francis Asbury, a Methodist circuit rider in this area in the 1790s. He established at least four hundred Methodist congregations in the Appalachians.

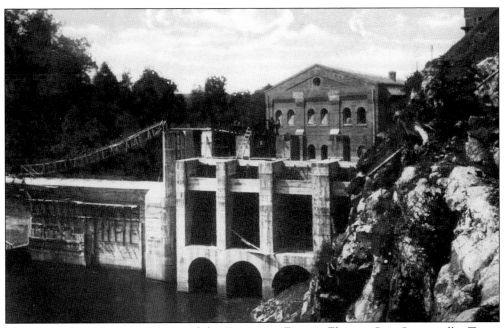

The Hydro Electric Power House of the Tennessee Eastern Electric Co., Greeneville, Tenn. This undated postcard illustrates one of the most important commodities—electric power—available in the Greeneville region.

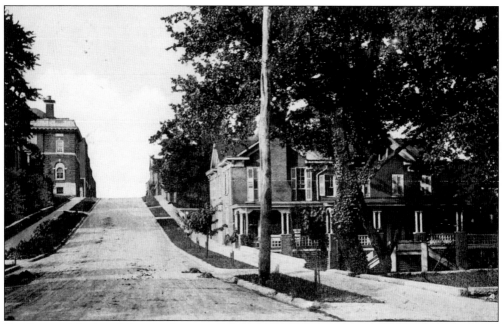

Residence of Andrew Johnson, Greeneville, Tenn. Andrew Johnson, seventeenth President of the United States, came to Greeneville when he was seventeen and opened a tailor shop. After entering local politics at a young age, he advanced in rank and prestige to the presidency. He bought his home on West Main Street in 1851.

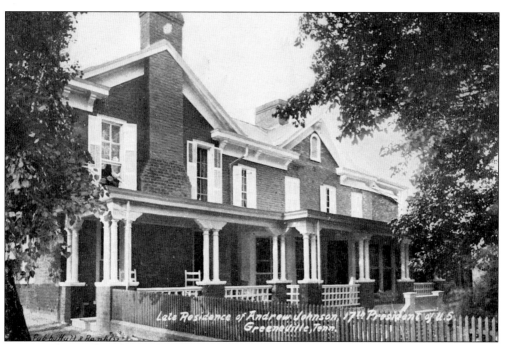

Late Residence of Andrew Johnson, Greeneville, Tenn. This picture gives a closer look at the Johnson residence. President Johnson came back to this home after his term in the White House, and he died here in 1875.

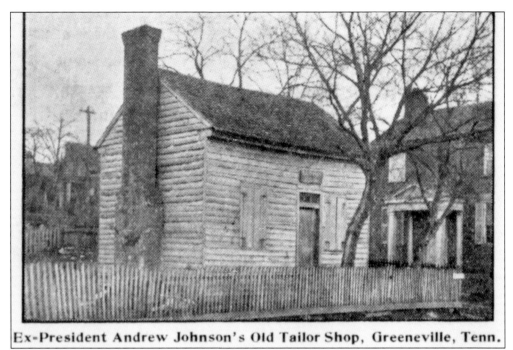

Ex-President Andrew Johnson's Old Tailor Shop, Greeneville, Tenn.

Ex-President Andrew Johnson's Old Tailor Shop, Greeneville, Tenn. This 1905 postcard shows the old building before a protective brick memorial was built over and around it. The wording "Ex-President" seems somewhat unusual.

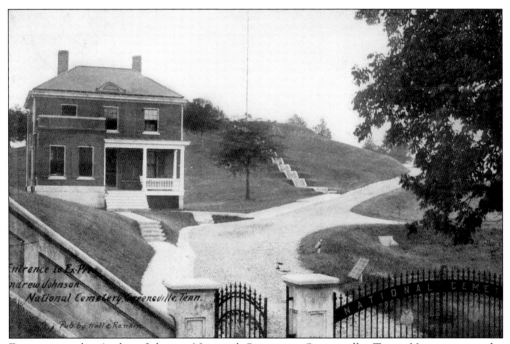

Entrance to the Andrew Johnson National Cemetery, Greeneville, Tenn. Visitors enter the gate on Monument Avenue and ascend the hill to the top, where Johnson's monument stands. He selected the spot himself. This postcard was mailed in 1913.

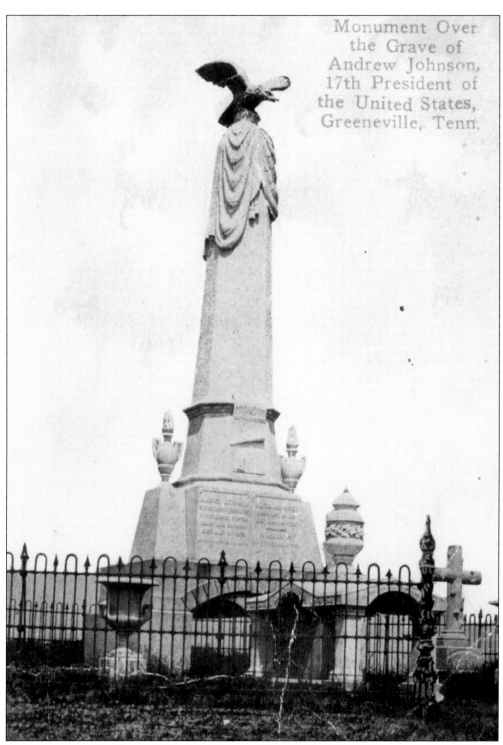

Monument Over
the Grave of
Andrew Johnson,
17th President of
the United States,
Greeneville, Tenn.

Monument over the Grave of Andrew Johnson, Greeneville, Tenn. The monument is 27 feet tall and topped by an eagle perched on a globe. President Johnson was the first to be buried in this cemetery; now veterans from all wars, from the Civil War to Vietnam, have joined him.

Eight

NEWPORT
Cocke County

Motoring south from Greeneville on Route 35 (321) past Parrottsville, we arrive 29 miles later at Newport. The town is located at the foot of the Great Smoky Mountains. Side streets drop down to the long, level main street that follows the valley of the Pigeon River. Across the river are high rocky bluffs.

In 1789 a colony of Pennsylvania Germans settled in this area along the northern bank of the French Broad River, the settlement becoming known as Dutch Bottoms. Sometime after 1797 the name was changed to Old Town, and then to New Port. When a new site on the Pigeon River was utilized for a court house, the residents accepted Newport on the Pigeon as the permanent seat of justice.

Newport is the home of Ben W. Hooper, governor of Tennessee from 1911 to 1915 and a member of the United States Railroad Labor Board from 1921 to 1925. Stokely Brothers, canners of vegetables, have their home office and factory here.

Newport has a number of notable buildings. The Rhea-Mims Hotel on Church Street was once considered one of the finest hotels on the Dixie Highway. It is built of stone, most of which was quarried from the hillside near the hotel. Millstones used by Indians embellish the porch at the front of the building. The Cocke County Memorial Building, a memorial to soldiers from the county in all wars, is located at the western end of Church Street. The building has an auditorium, a gymnasium, a library, and meeting rooms.

High Oaks Tulip Gardens at 218 North Street received its name from the tall oaks in front of the house. The gardens contain almost every known variety of tulip and one also finds here dwarf trees, shrubs, hollyhocks, and rock plants. The John Sevier Preserve, on the southwestern side of the city, is a tract of 125,000 acres with a valley containing 10,000 acres of virgin timber.

Historic houses of Newport include Beechwood Hall, Elm Hill, the Ellison-Yett House, Greenlawn, and O'Dell House, all of which are listed on the National Register of Historic Places. There are also many other business developments, churches, cemeteries, and homes reflecting the past events and experiences of Newport which invite the interest of tourists.

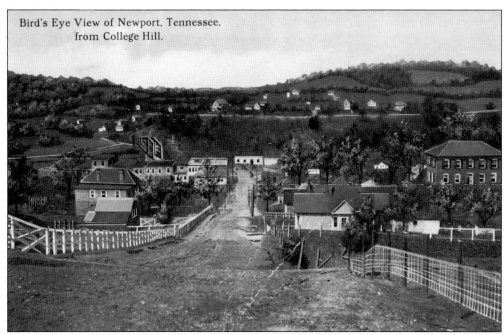

Bird's Eye View of Newport, Tennessee, from College Hill. Mailed in 1919, this card reads: "Just off from work—wish you were here for tomorrow. I am thinking of going to the country. Come go along."

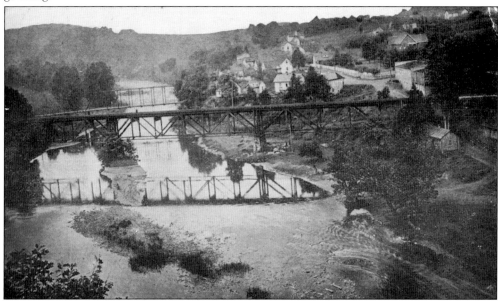

Bird's Eye View of East Part, Newport, Tenn. The stream seen here is the Pigeon River. This postcard gives us a good picture of Newport's interesting position, nestled against the bank. The sender of this card, mailed in 1919, writes: "Newport, the home of Gov. Ben Hooper, was one of our stopping places. We were honored by the Governor's presence while there. He introduced the speakers to a large audience. This was my first visit to Newport. It is a delightful place. The scenic grandeur of the place is charming. Wish you could visit the little queen of the Cumberlands."

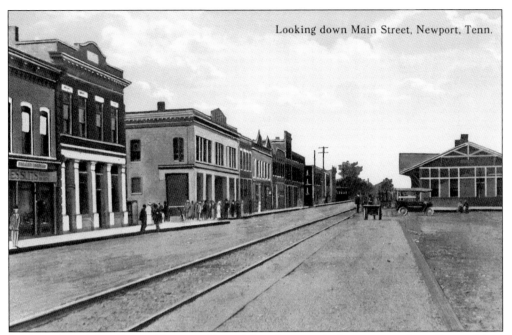

Looking down Main Street, Newport, Tenn. This photograph shows a typical small-town Main Street about 1920. Note the railroad tracks and depot at the right of the picture. One wonders whether the group of people on the corner is waiting for the next train.

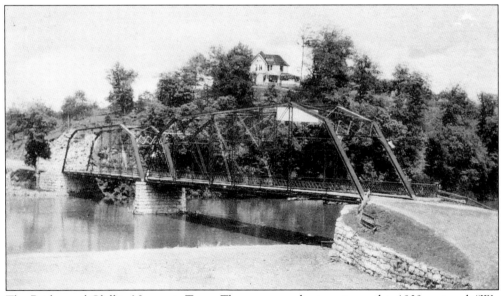

The Bridge and Cliff in Newport, Tenn. The correspondent wrote on this 1909 postcard: "We are in N.P. have bought several pigs are going to leave this evening Mr. G and my self struck a good friend he is helping us." Hog raising was an important enterprise in the Newport area.

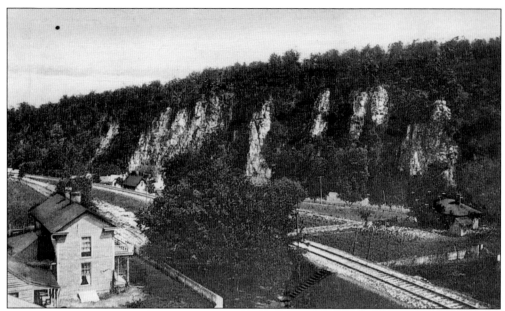

Along the Pigeon River in Newport, Tenn. In 1911 the sender of this card wrote: "Your letter came today. Thank you for the little folder and the information. This is the river on which I live and the house looks a lot like ours."

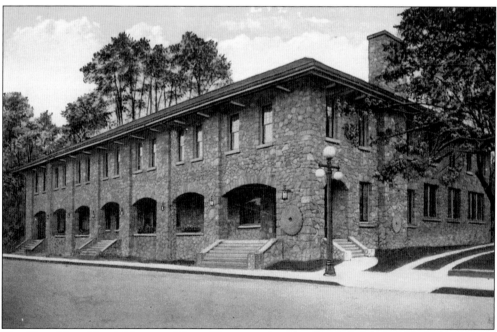

The Rhea-Mims Hotel, Newport, Tenn. This stone hotel was built with materials quarried from nearby hills. Indian millstones were used on the front and sides of the building.

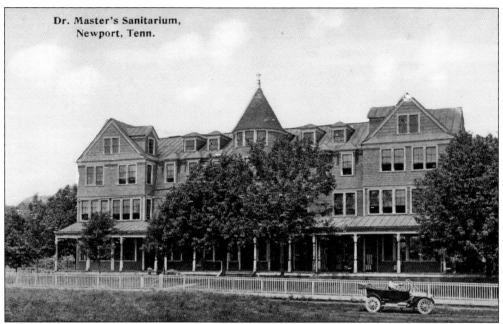

Dr. Master's Sanitarium,
Newport, Tenn.

Dr. Master's Sanatarium, Newport, Tenn. In 1913 when this postcard was mailed, the sender wrote: "Dear Uncle, Sorry we could not have stayed and visited with you for a day or two when there. Our time is always limited. You don't know how glad we were to see you. We realize that our near relatives will soon be gone. Am going to send you some pictures soon." By the 1920s the building was in use as the Cherokee Hotel.

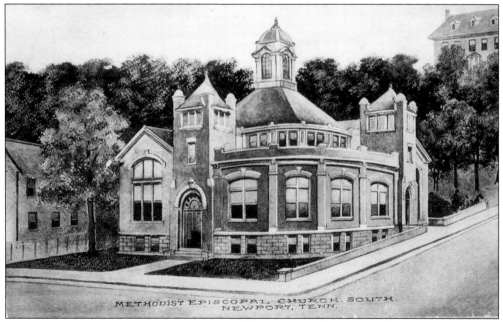

METHODIST EPISCOPAL CHURCH, SOUTH.
NEWPORT, TENN.

The Methodist Episcopal Church in South Newport, Tenn. On a sloping corner, this building presents an interesting rounded front, two towers, and a cupola. The sender of this card, mailed in 1910, wrote: "Here I am in the mts. having a fine time. Wish so much you were here. We must come down this winter if the Cleveland people don't go north."

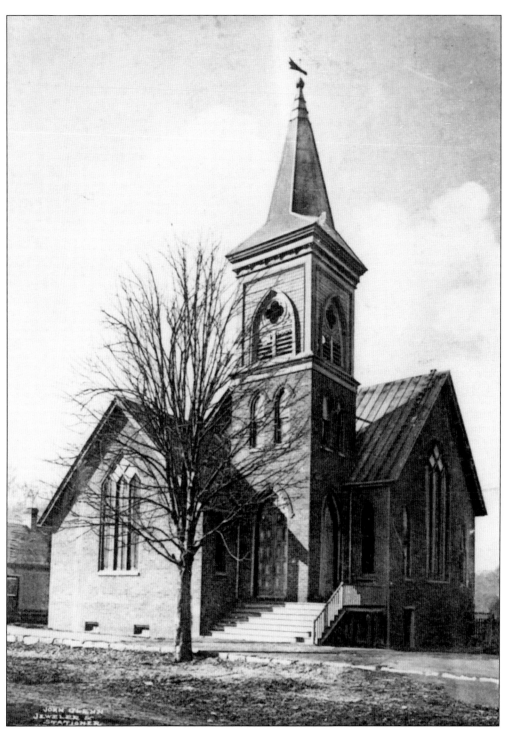

Presbyterian Church in Newport, Tenn. A small church, this edifice nevertheless projects inspiration with its lovely Gothic design. The correspondent in 1910 is matter-of-fact: "Got into my case after dinner and dont think will get through tomorrow evening but probably home Thursday. Kiss kiddies for me."

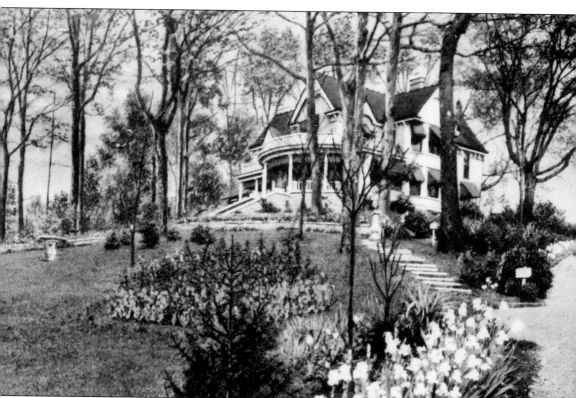

"High Oaks," the Home of Mrs. L.E. Duncan, Newport, Tenn. The extent of the beautiful grounds and flowers contained in Mrs. Duncan's domain is suggested by this photograph. The house shows Victorian architecture at its best.

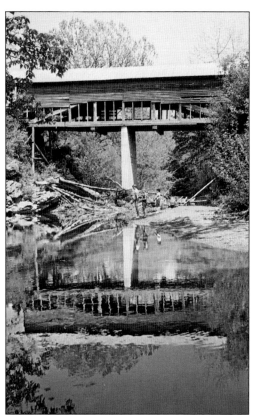

Pigeon Bridge, south of Newport, Tenn. The bridge is pictured as it appeared in 1969. Constructed in 1890, it is 64 feet long and consists of one span crossing the the Pigeon River just south of Newport. It is typical of many of the old covered bridges which are disappearing from American life.

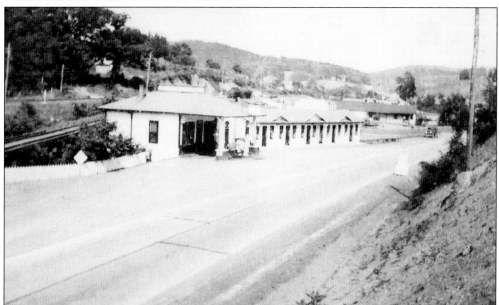

Front View of the Eureka Cabins and T & S Service Station, Newport, Tenn. Even though these "cabins" open directly on to the road, the management promises "Shower bath in every room—Purified city water—Private kitchen for tourists—lunch room in connection—We're always open." A 1930s vintage automobile can be seen in the distance.

Nine

DANDRIDGE
Jefferson County

The Dandridge area was first settled in 1782 by a group of Scotch-Irish. The county, named for Thomas Jefferson, lies between the French Broad and Holston Rivers. The town, on the northern bank of the French Broad, is the only city in the United States named for George Washington's wife, Martha Dandridge Custis.

Here, on January 16, 1864, the left wing of the Confederate Army under General Longstreet surprised Union forces under General Granger. After a brief skirmish, Longstreet's men drove their opponents back to Knoxville. A Dandridge woman invited the Confederate officers to her home, in which the Union commander had been a guest the night before. He had left a bottle of brandy, and from it the Confederate officers drank a satirical toast to him.

In the office of the county court clerk in Dandridge one may find the marriage bond between David Crockett and Polly Finley, as well as the record of an earlier license issued to Crockett and Margaret Elder, returned unused.

The Hynds House, built by Shadrack Inman as a wedding present for his daughter Elizabeth in 1844, is located half a block northwest of the court house. The site is that of an old still, famous for the quality of its whiskey. The house was used as a hospital by the Confederates after the siege of Knoxville.

The Soldiers' Monument northeast of the court house was erected on the site of the first Hopewell Presbyterian Church, whose congregation organized in 1785 and is still in existence. Nearby lie several other historic buildings and sites, among them the Branner Grist Mill (1850); the Dumplin Treaty Marker, commemorating the treaty with the Cherokees that opened up the country south of the French Broad to white settlers; and the Island Mound in the French Broad River.

Shepard's Inn, built in 1820 by the Shadrack Inman family, became a tavern and boardinghouse after the Civil War; it was then known as the Mitchell House. The Roper Tavern was built in 1817 and the Rogers-Miller House, with its elaborate Italianate porch, dates from 1860.

A number of historic homes have interesting stories to be told. Squirewood, built by Judge James Preston Swann in 1858, has a small hidden room accessed through a closet where the Swanns concealed a wounded Union soldier. The Samuel McSpadden House has attic portholes for guns, and a first floor with walls four-bricks thick. The Nina Harris House is of brick with a two-story portico topped by a pediment. These and other important sites which illuminate past events make Dandridge one of Tennessee's most revealing journeys into its history.

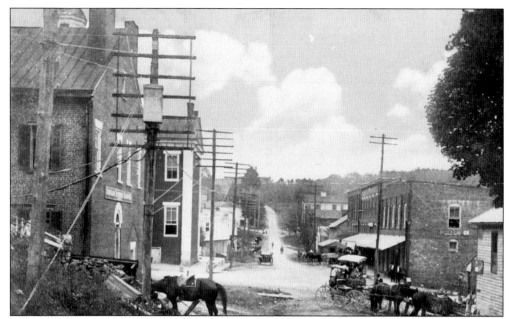

Main Street, Dandridge, Tenn. One has to guess at the time of this picture, but the primitive appearance of the street indicates a date prior to 1910. Horses and buggies predominate; one early automobile approaches.

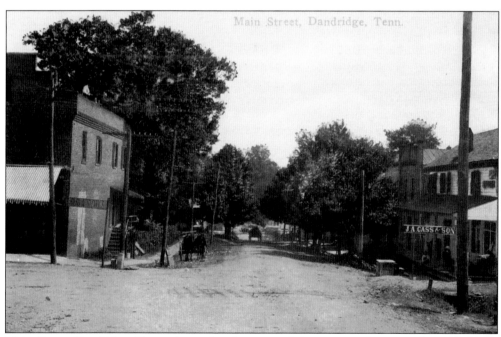

Main Street, Dandridge, Tenn. A tree-lined section of the street is shown, with two business establishments named. At the left we see "Gass and Nichols" and on the right "J.A. Gass and Son." Two horses harnessed to a wagon stand at the side. The date is about 1910.

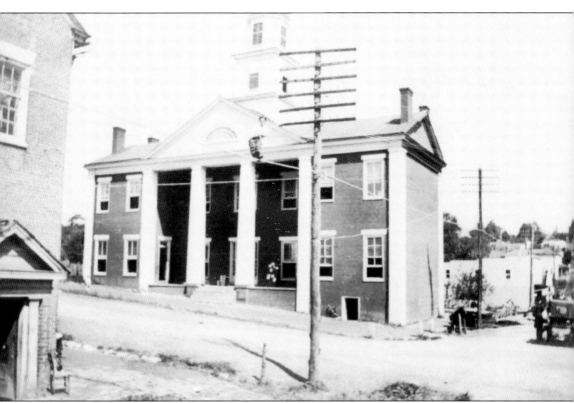

Jefferson County Court House, Dandridge, Tenn. The court house is located on Main Street in the center of the historic district. A very early court house, it features Greek Revival design. The sender of the 1912 postcard says: "Kiddie you get the Courthouse. Was built in 1845. Isn't that 'some old'?" (Postcard courtesy of Paul Garland.)

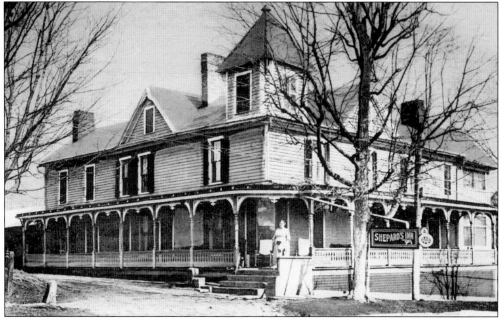

Shepard's Inn, Dandridge, Tenn. Shepard's Inn was built in 1820. It became a tavern and boarding house after the Civil War, when it was known as the Mitchell House. Some picture postcards show the same building with the Mitchell House name as identification.

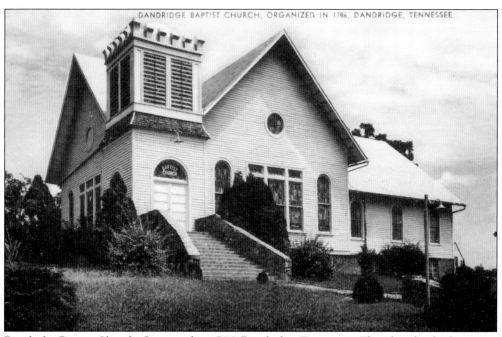

DANDRIDGE BAPTIST CHURCH, ORGANIZED IN 1786, DANDRIDGE, TENNESSEE

Dandridge Baptist Church, Organized in 1786, Dandridge, Tennessee. This church, also known as First Baptist Church, is the third oldest church in Tennessee in continued existence. The building in the picture was first used in 1845; it was subsequently abandoned for a new location.

Ten

KIMBERLIN HEIGHTS
Knox County

The Kimberlin Heights community, on the south bank of the French Broad River, was founded in 1786. It was first known as Greene's Station, and later as Manifold's Station; still later it was called Gap Creek. In 1787 Jacob Kimberlin, a Revolutionary War soldier, discovered lead here, and some have said that he also discovered silver on the spot where Johnson Bible College now stands.

In 1859 Gap Creek was a post office in Knox County; however, by 1887 this name was changed to Kimberlin Heights. The post office was located in the home of Dr. Ashley Sidney Johnson, grandson of Jacob Kimberlin, who had purchased the old Kimberlin place and had established a correspondence Bible College. In 1893 he opened the Johnson Bible College here to train ministers for the Christian Church. He was president of the college until his death; he is buried on the campus.

Besides the college there is an elementary school located here and two churches: a Christian church and the Forest Grove Baptist Church. Adjacent communities are New Hopewell, 2 miles below, and Seven Islands, about 2 miles above the college.

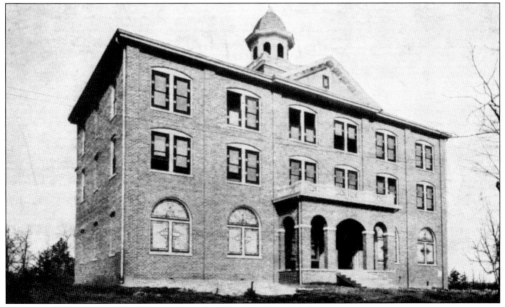

Main Building, School of Evangelists, Kimberlin Heights, Tenn.

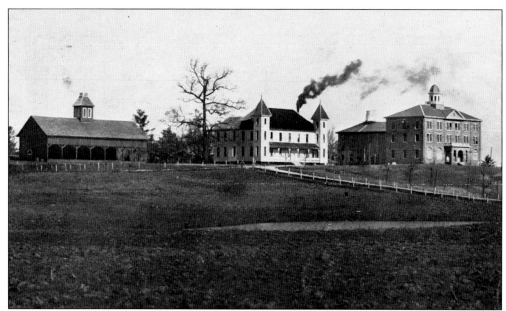

Johnson Bible College, Kimberlin Heights, Tenn. Johnson Bible College was founded in 1893 to educate men and women in religious vocations. The correspondent here in 1909 writes: "Many many thanks I give you additionally. Dinner and dessert April 25th. This makes two meals, the other being breakfast April 24th. We appreciate your interest in these young men."

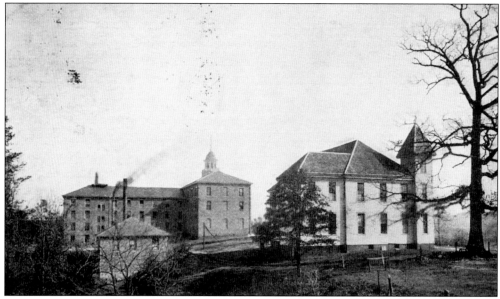

A side view of the School of Evangelists, Kimberlin Heights, Tenn. A 1910 postcard reveals the sender's happy enthusiasm: "Fudge and Divinity Fudge! Did ever mortals taste candy so good. I have my serious doubts. The boys that were so fortunate as to get a taste certainly can thank their lucky stars. All of them said to thank you and say they appreciated it. As for me, I can't tell you how much I enjoyed it. A thousand thanks—it was certainly par excellence."

Eleven

KNOXVILLE
Knox County

Knoxville is located on the Tennessee River, which is formed 4 miles east of the downtown section by the junction of the Holston and French Broad Rivers. The city extends fan-wise from the river banks into the nearby hills, with the Chilhowee and the Great Smoky Mountains in the distance.

The business section is on a plateau of 240 acres. Gay Street, the main thoroughfare, has both modern and historic buildings. A bus terminal is in the mid-section of Gay Street; one block west one finds Market Square, where a free market for farmers has existed since 1897. Industries are scattered throughout the city: marble mills, sand and gravel industries, iron and steel, and lumber yards. A large wholesale district is located near the Southern Railway. Beautiful modern homes may be found in Sequoyah Hills and Holston Hills; however, there are many old Victorian houses elsewhere in the city.

Knoxville is unique in many ways and has historically had a number of interesting practices. For example, Knoxville was the only city in the United States where one could stop a streetcar to drop a letter in its outside mail box. Mail collections from streetcars and busses were established here by the post office in 1914.

Knoxville is known for the Tennessee Valley Authority (TVA); established here in 1933 to enhance navigation, soil conservation, power distribution, and to control floods, it brought in more than one thousand new families. The TVA has had widespread economic effect on Knoxville and eastern Tennessee, and there is a national interest in its work, resulting in an increase in tourists.

In 1786 James White, having explored the country, built a log cabin here and became the first permanent settler in Knoxville. Later he added three more cabins and connected the four by a high palisade of logs, making a frontier outpost known as White's Fort. During the next five years, settlers flocked to the Knoxville area, and White's Fort became a repair and restocking point for westbound wagon trains.

William Blount, commissioned governor of the Territory South of the River Ohio, came to Tennessee in 1790 and established his headquarters at White's settlement. The Treaty of Holston was then made with the Cherokees. At Blount's suggestion, Captain White laid out streets, and the new town was named Knoxville in honor of Major General Henry Knox, secretary of war. It became the county seat in 1792.

In 1793 the First Presbyterian Church was organized, and a ferry service to the settlements south of the Tennessee River organized. In 1795 a post office with semi-monthly mail service to Washington was established, and a wagon road to Nashville was completed. On June 1, 1796, Tennessee was admitted into the Union, with Knoxville as its first state capital. The state government was moved to Nashville in 1812.

For the first decade, Knoxville was a frontier town where pioneers stopped to buy supplies on their way west. In 1790 a certain James Weir described the scene in Knoxville on County Court Day. He witnessed "men jesting, singing, swearing . . . half naked Negroes playing on their banjoes . . . Whiskey and peach brandy were cheap . . . Indians, woodsmen, gamblers" and his "soul shrank to hear the horrid oaths and dreadful indignities."

By the mid-nineteenth century the railway came to Knoxville, making communications with Chattanooga, Nashville, and Bristol swift and easy, and promoting the growth of industry in the area and the development of the city itself. The Civil War arrested the growth of the city; the damage to Knoxville properties was enormous.

The majority of East Tennesseans were loyal to the Union, but because of this a Confederate army of occupation was sent here early in 1861, establishing its headquarters in Knoxville. About 1,500 Union sympathizers were arrested, tried, and sent to prisons farther south. All Confederate troops were withdrawn in August 1863 and mobilized in Chattanooga. About the same time Major General A.E. Burnside arrived with twenty thousand Union soldiers. In November 1863 Gen. James A. Longstreet, with fifteen thousand men, attacked Burnside; he was, however, defeated and moved back toward Morristown. All Knoxville public buildings and many private homes were either destroyed by shellfire or were badly damaged by troop quartering.

Knoxville recovered rapidly after the war, and the next thirty years saw a blossoming of industries, an increase in railroad transportation, and an influx of new residents. The city expanded from 3.9 to 26.4 square miles. Industrial enterprises at this time were producing cotton textiles, marble, hardwood furniture, porcelain manufacture, flour, cement products, steel, agricultural implements, and thermostatic control devices.

There are many places of historical importance in Knoxville. The site of Blount College, on the southeast corner of South Gay Street and West Clinch Avenue, is marked by a bronze plaque on the Gay Street side of the Burwell Building. Blount College, named for Governor William Blount and chartered in 1794, was the third institution of higher learning west of the Alleghenies and was co-educational from the beginning. Barbara Blount, daughter of the governor, was among its early graduates. In 1806 Blount College assumed the new name of East Tennessee College; in 1826 it moved to new property purchased on "The Hill"; in 1840 the name changed again, to the East Tennessee University; and in 1879 it became the University of Tennessee. Since then its growth has been steady. It offers over one hundred areas of study, research opportunities, and public service and cultural events. The main campus extends along Cumberland Avenue with more than one hundred buildings, many of them notable examples of significant architectural styles. Divisions of the university are located in Memphis, Martin, Nashville, and Chattanooga.

The First Presbyterian Church, at 620 State Street, of neo-classic design and constructed of yellow brick with limestone trim, was completed in 1901. It houses the oldest church organization in Knoxville and is the third building on the site. The first was finished in 1816; the second in 1852. During the war it was used by the Union Army as a barracks, hospital quarters for refugees, and a school for black children. William Blount, James White, and Dr. Samuel Garrick (the first president of the university) are buried in the graveyard.

The Hunter-Kennedy House at 216 E. Church Avenue, erected by James Kennedy of Pennsylvania in 1820, is a two-story brick structure with a handsome cherry staircase leading to large bedrooms upstairs. Mr. Kennedy's slaves produced almost all the products needed by the community. The remains of a gristmill and a smokehouse are reminders of the slave plantation. The house is now privately owned.

The Jackson House at 1000 State Street was built in 1800 of red clay bricks and is well preserved. It has thick, ivy-covered walls, a small front porch with an iron grill balcony, and ornate exterior details. A secret stairway is built into a closet in an upper-story room. Of late Georgian design, the house works as a neat complement to Blount Mansion nearby.

The Blount Mansion, at State Street and Hill Avenue, is the first frame house built west of the Alleghenies. It was built in 1792 by Governor William Blount. Of Georgian Colonial design, it has a two-story central portion between one-story wings. The central block contains a passage and a parlor, the east wing a drawing room, and the west wing a chamber or office. The large rooms have hand-made mantelpieces, chair rails, and wide panelled doors. They contain a variety of irreplaceable pioneer furniture, portraits, pewter, and china. An old fashioned garden surrounds the house. This property is one of the most important tourist attractions in Knoxville.

Chisholm's Tavern at 217 Front Avenue was built in 1792 by Captain John Chisholm, a soldier of fortune. It was built of logs covered by hand-hewn weatherboards and the foundation and cellar walls were 3 feet thick. The interior woodwork was heart pine and the great room had a 6-foot fireplace opening. The first Masonic lodge of Knoxville, with Governor John Sevier as worshipful master, is believed to have held its early meetings here. The building, located on a steep, sloping hillside overlooking the Tennessee River, was Chisholm's home as well as his tavern. In the early days it was famous for its food and hospitality. Chisholm's Tavern was demolished in 1966.

The Knox County Court House at West Main Avenue between South Gay and Market Streets is a massive, square, two-story, steel frame Queen Anne structure faced with brick and marble, and is decorated with terra-cotta friezes in the Victorian style. Designed by Palliser & Palliser of New York, it was erected in 1885. A marble arch at the entrance to the grounds honors Knoxville's family physician Dr. John Mason Boyd, who practiced here for more than fifty years. A stone marker designates the site of the military blockhouse built in 1793. Two other monuments on the grounds mark the graves of John Sevier and his second wife. A stone marker 100 feet south of the Sevier monument commemorates the Treaty of the Holston, signed on July 2, 1791.

The Lyric Theater at 802 South Gay Street was built in 1871 by Peter Staub. Formally opened in 1872 as Staub's Theatre, it has seen stage plays, musicals, and wrestling matches in its day. By the 1930s it had declined a good deal from its former elegance. It was demolished in 1956.

The Lawson McGhee Library at 217 Market Street was the second building occupied by the library since its establishment in 1885. Of modified Georgian Colonial design, it was built of white brick and terra-cotta materials. Designed by Grant B. Miller, it opened its doors in 1917. Part of its holdings included the C.M. McClung Historical Collection, which consists of about six thousand volumes of history and genealogy of the Southern states and can be said to be one of the finest collections of early books, maps, and documents in the South. The 217 Market Street library building was demolished, and the new library opened in 1971 at 500 West church Avenue. The McClung Collection is now housed at the East Tennessee Historical Society at 600 Market Street, in the building once known as the Post Office and Custom House.

The Market House, on Market Street between Wall and Union Avenues, was constructed in 1897 of red brick trimmed with white Knoxville marble. The stalls inside the Market House were leased to the merchants, and in the center aisle 104 tables were allotted free to farm women for the display of their produce. The free curb market outside the building accommodated many more farmers who lined up their wagons or trucks from which to display and sell produce.

Market Square forms a town within a town. In its heyday, it was a bustling, raucous spot. The women who ran the boarding houses on the second floors of the buildings around the square would descend to the street and clang hand bells to announce noontime lunch. A meal in one of these houses would cost 15¢ for "all you could eat," and a Western at one of the two movie houses on the square would cost 10¢. Unfortunately, the Market House burned in 1960. A pedestrian mall now stands on the site.

The Park House at 422 West Cumberland Avenue, built of brownish-red brick in post-Colonial style, is L-shaped and two-storied, with a narrow arcaded and latticed porch in the angle of the ell. John Sevier began the house in 1798, but he abandoned the construction when it was only half completed. James Park, who became mayor of Knoxville, bought and completed the house. It is now owned by the Knoxville Academy of Medicine and is used as a medical museum and a meeting place.

The Dickinson-Atkins House at 518 Main Avenue, begun by Perez Dickinson in 1830, was purchased and remodeled in 1901 by C. Brown Atkins, a Knoxville manufacturer. This two-story white post-Colonial house stood far back from the street at the end of a spacious lawn and garden. The beautiful portico was added in 1905. The house was demolished in 1950, but its portico was bought and added to the Kingsport home of Harvey Brooks.

The Church Street Methodist Episcopal Church, at the southwest corner of West Main Avenue and Broadway (Henley Street) was completed in 1930. It is of neo-Gothic design with exterior walls faced with quartz stone; the trim is Indiana limestone. Interior pews are made of oak and the aisles are paved with sandstone. Designed by Barber and McMurry of Knoxville, it excels in its high standards of design, detailing, and craftmanship.

The Henley Street Bridge spans the Tennessee at the south end of Broadway (Henley Street). It is 1,800 feet long and 300 feet above the low water mark. It was ready for service in January 1932.

Tyson Memorial House at 830 Sixteenth Street is a large residence of Georgian Colonial design. Once the home of Colonel L.D. Tyson, a wealthy manufacturer of Knoxville and, in later years, a United States Senator, it now houses the University of Tennessee Alumni Affairs Office and is used as a recreational and religious center for students.

Bleak House at 2800 Kingston Pike, named for the novel by Charles Dickens, is a two-story brick building painted gray. General Longstreet made his headquarters here during the siege of Knoxville. Union artillery fired upon the house and damaged it somewhat; a number of minie balls are still embedded in the walls.

Knoxville College is one of the oldest institutions for black education in the South. At the time of its establishment, about one hundred black children and adults attended class in a one-room abandoned grocery store. Today more than three hundred students use twenty-eight buildings on a beautiful campus of 20 acres, part of the 90-acre tract owned by the college. The red brick buildings, three and four stories high, are trimmed in wood and stone. The campus occupies the site of the Confederate encampment under General Longstreet during the siege of Knoxville. Some of the most outstanding buildings are the Administration Building, the Carnegie Library, and the MacMillan Memorial Chapel, the latter erected in 1913.

National and Old Gray Cemeteries are located on Broadway between Tyson and Cooper Streets, and adjoin each other. National Cemetery, founded by the government in 1863 for the interment of Union soldiers killed in East Tennessee, also has the graves of Spanish-American and World War I veterans. In Old Gray Cemetery there are many graves of prominent people, including Governor W.G. (Parson) Brownlow, Horace Maynard, L.D. Tyson, and William Gibbs McAdoo.

Ramsey House on Thorngrove Road was built in 1797 by Colonel F.A. Ramsey, the surveyor who accompanied Captain James White on his exploring expedition in 1783. The architect was Thomas Hope of London, who had been brought to the United States in 1752 by Ralph Izard to build his now-famous house in Charleston. The Ramsey House is a two-story building in Gothic style with long narrow windows. It was built of red granite, trimmed in pure blue limestone, and ornamented with elaborately finished cornices. In 1800 it was the most costly and admired building in Tennessee.

At the quarry and power plant of the Appalachian Marble Company, one of the largest quarries in East Tennessee, there are three types of marble—gray, pink, and rose. The beautiful pink marble is light in color and has flecks of red; it is very decorative and takes a high polish. The quarry dates from 1869, when it was opened to furnish marble for the old Knoxville Post Office and Custom House at West Clinch and Market. Every color of marble except white can be found in Tennessee.

In the western part of Knoxville we find several grand old homes worthy of note. On Middlebrook Pike there is Middlebrook, built in 1845; Lonas House, now a museum of the Tennessee frontier; and States View, which once stood on the 2,000-acre plantation of Charles McClung. There is also the Old Mabry Place, built in 1851 by George Mabry, the son of Joseph A. Mabry.

Passing through Farragut (named in honor of David Glasgow Farragut, the first man to have the rank of admiral in the American Navy), we follow Lowes Ferry Pike to Pleasant Hill Cemetery, where there is a monument to Archibald Roane, governor of Tennessee after John Sevier. Lowe's Ferry was operated near this point for nearly one hundred years by the family of Abraham Lowe; it was a very important communication link for troops during the Civil War.

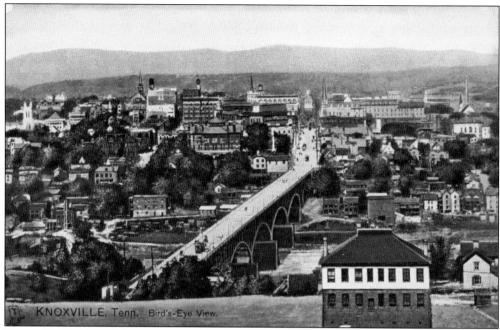

Knoxville, Tenn., Bird's-Eye View. This view shows the city as the visitor would have seen it as he was about to cross the Gay Street Bridge. The card was sent on July 11, 1908, for the birthday of Norman Francis Main.

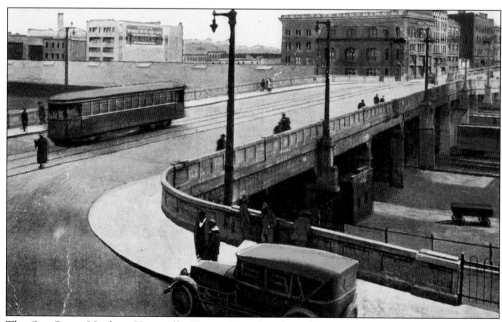

The Gay Street Viaduct, Knoxville, Tenn. Completed in 1919, the Gay Street Viaduct over the railroad tracks accommodated all kinds of traffic—street cars, horses and buggies, automobiles, and pedestrians. Across the viaduct we see the Hall-Tate Clothing Company.

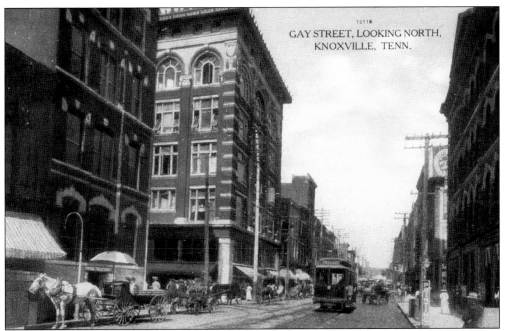

Gay Street looking North, Knoxville, Tenn. An early view, about 1912, shows the corner of Gay and Union, with Miller's department store prominent at left center. Transportation at this time centered around horse-drawn vehicles and the trolley.

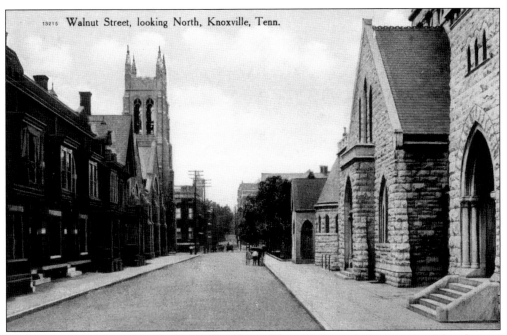

Walnut Street looking North, Knoxville, Tenn. The old Second Presbyterian Church is at left (on this site between 1906 and 1957) and St. John's Episcopal Church is on the right. St. John's, built in 1892, remains a prestigious downtown landmark.

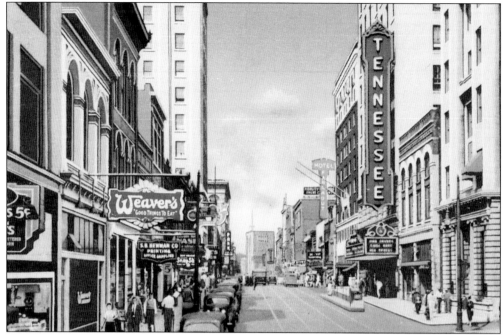

Gay Street looking North, Knoxville, Tenn. The Tennessee Theater, built in 1928, can be seen in this view. The Farragut Hotel is just beyond (look for the two flagpoles).

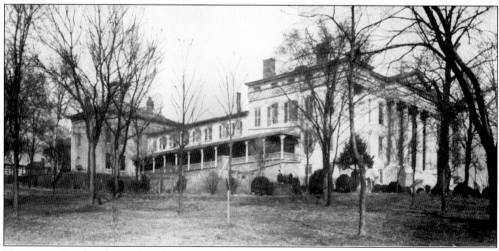

Tennessee Deaf and Dumb School, Knoxville, Tenn. Although the school was established in 1844, this building was not erected until 1851. It was used for the school until 1924, when the school was moved to Island Home and the building became City Hall.

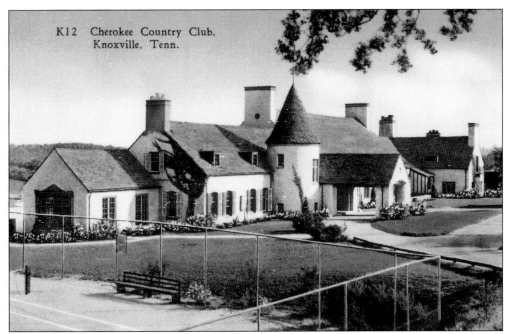

Cherokee Country Club, Knoxville, Tenn. Located on property 4 miles west of the city on Lyon's View Pike, the club overlooks the Horseshoe Bend of the Tennessee River. The second building on this site, it was built in 1928 after the architectural designs of Baumann and Baumann.

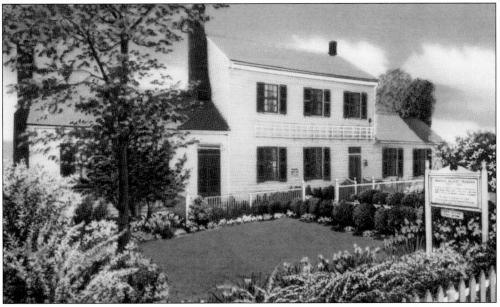

The William Blount Mansion, Knoxville, Tenn. The "mansion," erected in 1792, was one of the first frame houses built west of the Alleghenies. After many decades of gradual deterioration, the house was bought by a group of civic-minded Knoxvillians and restored as a historic landmark.

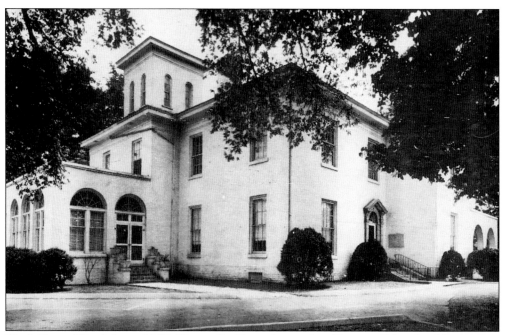

Bleak House (Confederate Hall), Knoxville, Tenn. Located on Kingston Pike, this fifteen-room antebellum mansion of hand-made brick was built by Robert Armstrong for his bride in 1856. In 1863 it served as General Longstreet's headquarters.

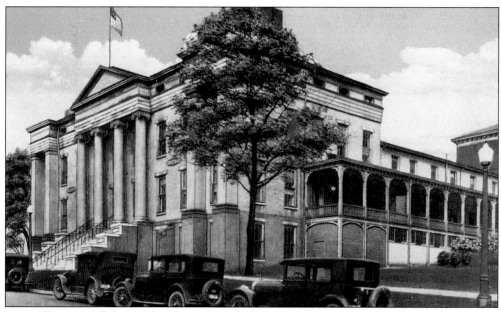

Knoxville City Hall. Located at the corner of Henley and Western, this building is an imposing example of Greek Revival style. It was used during the Civil War as a hospital by both Confederates and Federals.

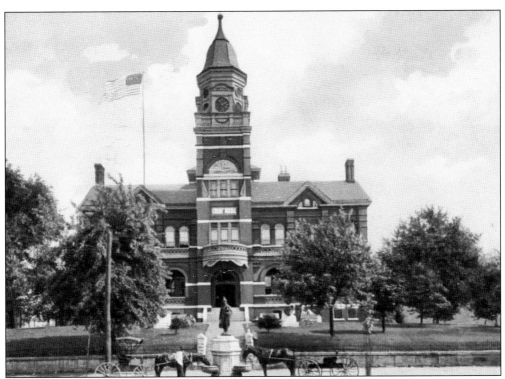

The Knox County Court House, Knoxville, Tenn. The Knox County Court House is bound by Main, Gay, Prince (Market), and Hill Streets. An impressive Queen Anne brick structure, it was built in 1885 by Palliser & Palliser of New York.

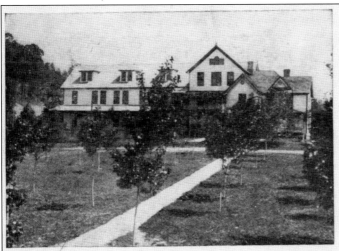

Whittle Springs, Tennessee. Located north of Knoxville. An ideal place to spend the Summer. Electric Lights, Baths. Modern conveniences. Telephone and Telegraph connections. Cuisine unexcelled. Whittle Springs water granted the Highest Award at St. Louis Exposition, 1904.

Rates $8.00 to $12.00 per week

Write for Catalogue.
Correspondence Solicited.

Altitude One Thousand Five Hundred Feet.

Address WHITTLE SPRINGS COMPANY, WHITTLE SPRINGS, E. TENNESSEE.

Whittle Springs, Tennessee. This advertising postcard shows the first Whittle Springs Hotel in north Knoxville about 1906. It was a summer resort for those who could afford the prices and who wanted to partake of the Whittle Springs water. It burned in 1919 and was replaced by a more luxurious hotel.

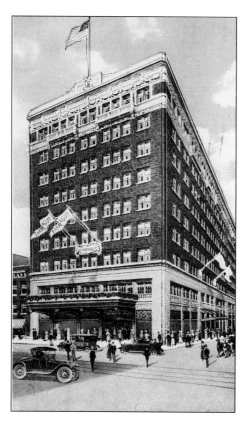

Hotel Farragut, Knoxville, Tenn. When the Hotel Farragut opened in 1919, its management went to great lengths to advertise that it was fireproof because the Imperial Hotel, previously on this site, had burned. The correspondent here, in 1920, writes: "Friend Chas: This is one of the many beautiful hotels in this city. Business is good here, and everyone seems to have plenty of money. Come South, young man!"

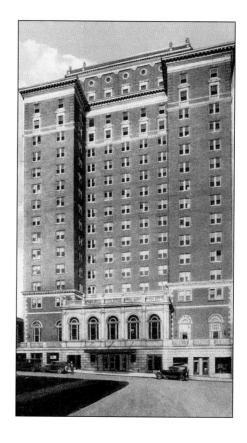

The Andrew Johnson Hotel, Knoxville, Tenn. Originally called the Tennessee Terrace, the Andrew Johnson replaced several fine homes on South Gay Street just across from the court house. It operated successfully during the Depression and was home to about one hundred permanent residents.

Knoxville Banking and Trust Co. Located on the southeast corner of Gay and Clinch (the former site of Blount College), this was Knoxville's tallest building in 1908. Later C.B. Atkin purchased it, doubled its size, and named it the Burwell Building. In 1928 the Tennessee Theater opened in its newer section.

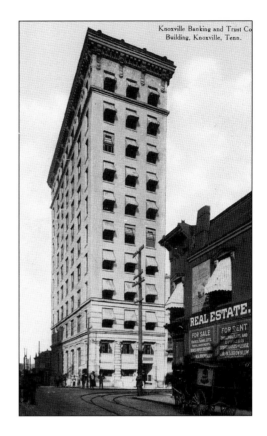

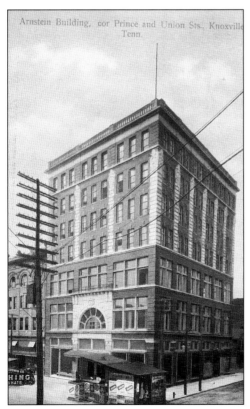

The Arnstein Building, Knoxville, Tenn. On the corner of Prince (Market) and Union, this seven-story "skyscraper" was built in 1905 and became one of the South's quality stores. It was the first steel-frame building erected in Knoxville. After the store closed in 1928, the premises were taken over by the Tennessee Valley Authority in the 1930s.

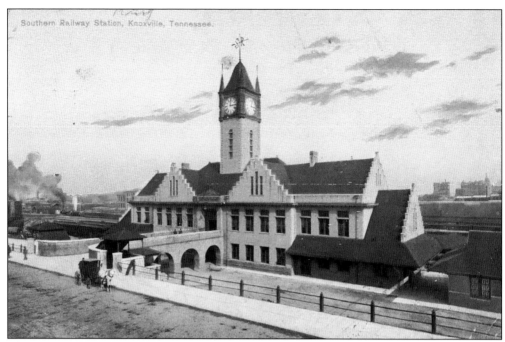

The Southern Railway Station, Knoxville, Tenn. A beautiful gray stone building with a clock tower, the Southern Station was located at the north end of the Gay Street Viaduct. Built in 1904, it served railway passengers until 1970, when such traffic ceased in Knoxville. The tower has since been removed and the building used for other business.

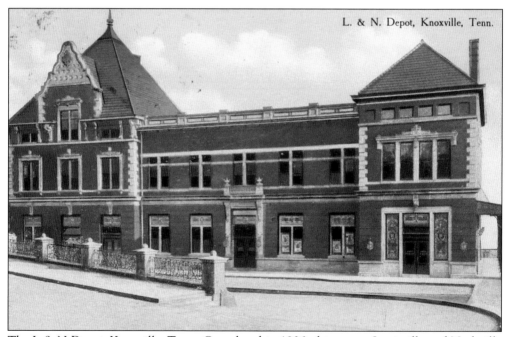

The L & N Depot, Knoxville, Tenn. Completed in 1906, this ornate Louisville and Nashville passenger depot became a landmark. It had beautiful stained glass windows and tile floors laid in Oriental carpet patterns.

The Y.M.C.A., Knoxville, Tenn. This building
at State and Commerce was the first building
in the city devoted to the cause. The later
YMCA at Locust and Clinch dates from 1929.

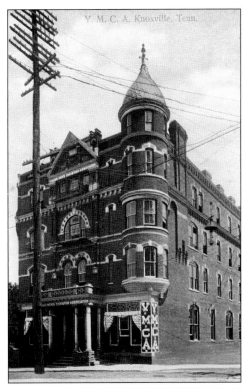

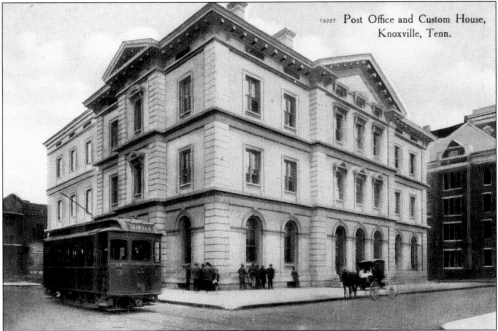

Post Office and Custom House, Knoxville, Tenn. Built in 1874, the old Post Office is Italianate
in design and is solidly constructed with iron beams and exterior walls of local marble. One of
the first buildings in Knoxville to be designed by a professional architect, it is located at Clinch
and Market Streets.

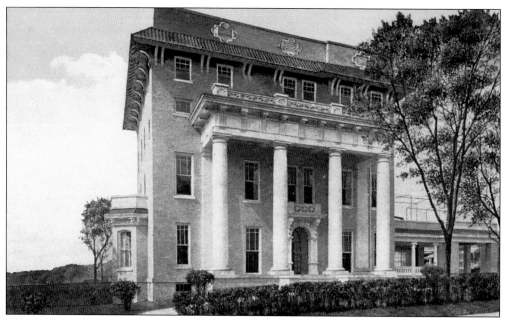

Masonic Temple, Knoxville, Tenn. Designed by Knoxville architect Joseph F. Baumann in 1872, this building was the home of Charles McClung McGhee, the donor of the Lawson McGhee Library. In 1907, after Mr. McGhee's death, it was altered to serve as a Masonic temple.

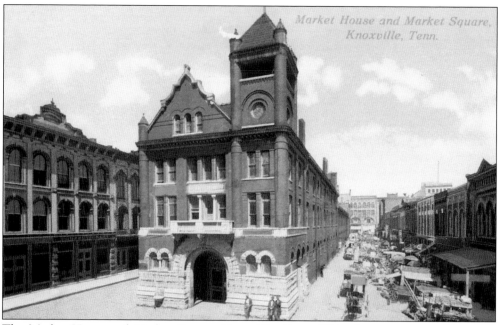

The Market House and Market Square, Knoxville, Tenn. This place, unique in Knoxville history, was busy for decades. Built in 1897, the Market House offered a world of produce, meat, and bakery products; outside on the square, carts lined up to offer more.

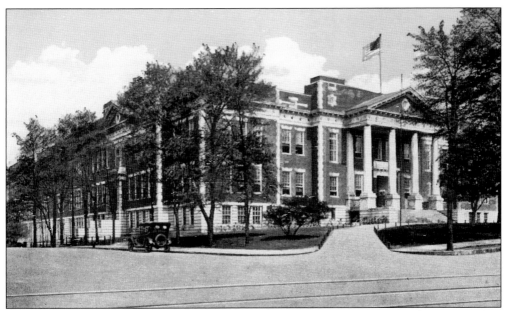

Knoxville High School. Opened in 1910, Knoxville High was the most prestigious school in the city for forty-one years, known for its "college preparation" courses. The building's classical facade is well complemented with Tennessee marble.

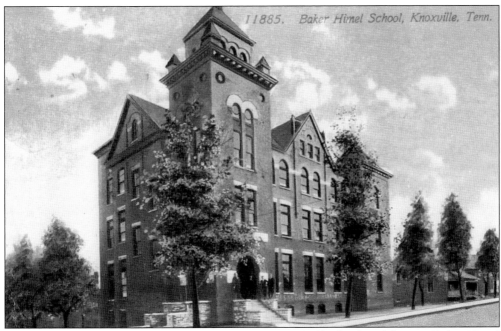

11885. Baker Himel School, Knoxville, Tenn.

Baker-Himel School, Knoxville, Tenn. One of the "grand old schools" of the city, Baker-Himel was a college preparatory school for boys located on Highland Avenue. Opened in 1889, the school closed in 1913.

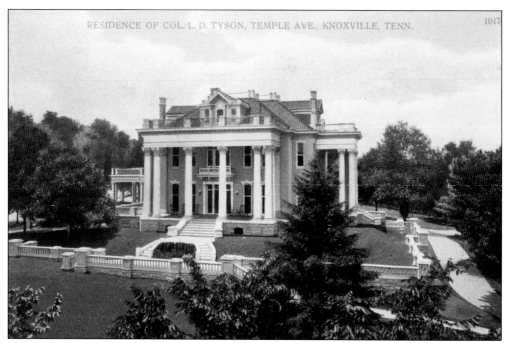

Residence of Colonel L.D. Tyson, Temple Avenue, Knoxville, Tenn. Tyson came to the University of Tennessee as a commandant of cadets. The house in this postcard dates from 1907, when Tyson's original frame house was faced with brick and ornamented with classical elements by architect George Barber.

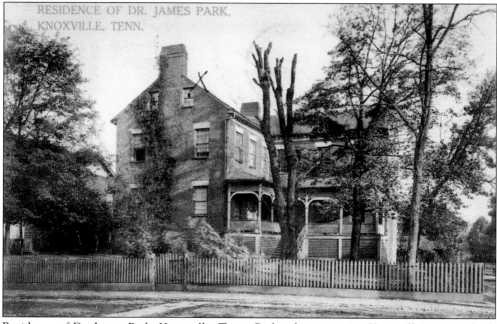

Residence of Dr. James Park, Knoxville, Tenn. Park, who was twice Knoxville's mayor, built this house in 1812. The Park family lived here for three generations. This postcard was mailed on November 29, 1911, from a member of the Park family to a relative; she marked with an 'X' the location of her playroom.

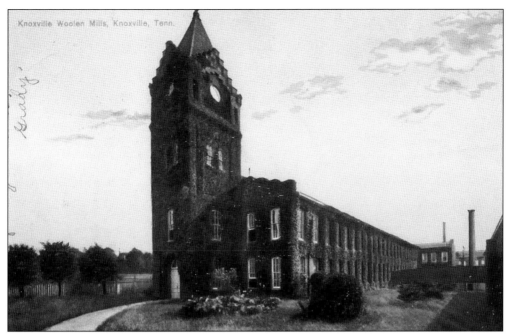

Knoxville Woolen Mills, Knoxville, Tenn. By 1884 this enterprise had become Knoxville's largest employer. In 1911 it changed hands and became Appalachian Mills, an operation that was very successful in producing men's ribbed knitted underwear.

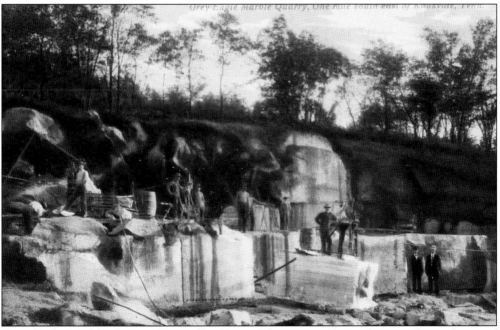

Grey Eagle Marble Quarry, Knoxville, Tenn. This quarry, located one mile southeast of Knoxville, Tennessee, quarries twenty varieties of marble. The second-largest marble quarry in the United States and one of the world's largest plants for producing finished marble are in Knoxville.

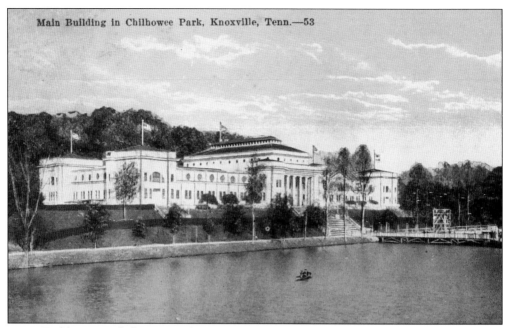

Main Building in Chilhowee Park, Knoxville, Tenn. Built in 1913 for the Appalachian Exposition of that year, this huge structure overlooked the lake from the land on which the Jacobs Building now stands. A traveler in 1921 writes: "A warm and clear day. Good road most all day. Came through Chattanooga this a.m.—going to camp in an old house tonight."

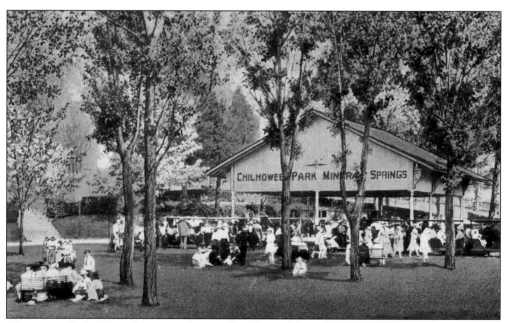

Chilhowee Park Mineral Springs, Knoxville, Tenn. Mineral springs were popular gathering places in the first decades of the century. The one in Chilhowee Park was a competitor of the well-known Fountain City springs.

110

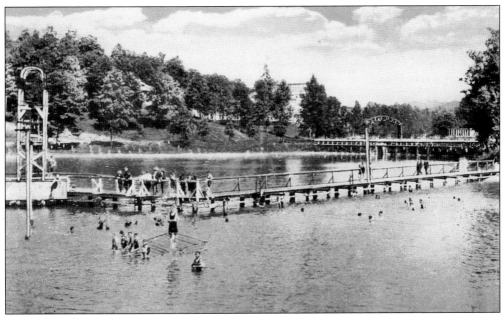

Bathing Beach and Lake at Chilhowee Park, Knoxville, Tenn. Swimming and boating were two popular recreations at the Park about 1910. The big exhibition building can be seen in the background.

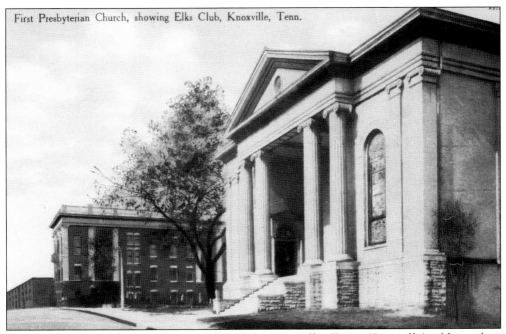

First Presbyterian Church, showing Elks Club, Knoxville, Tenn. Knoxville's oldest urban church sits on land reserved by James White in 1796. In its adjacent graveyard lie founder James White, Samuel Carrick, the first pastor, and William Blount, governor of the Southwest Territory.

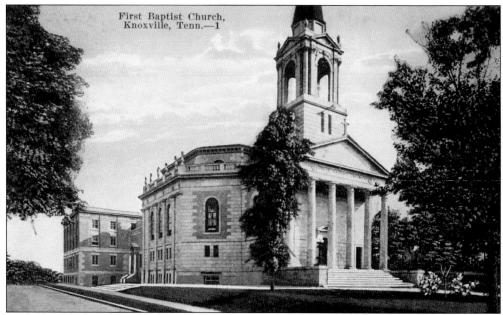

First Baptist Church, Knoxville, Tenn. One of the finest classical buildings in Knoxville, First Baptist is located on the site of the McClung House on Main Street. Built in the 1920s, it is constructed of gray brick and Indiana limestone, and cost a total of $500,000.

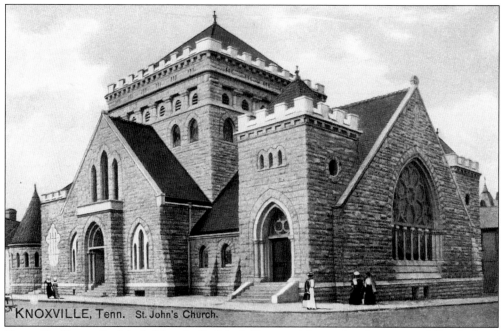

Knoxville, Tenn., St. John's Church. St. John's Episcopal, located at the corner of Cumberland and Walnut Streets, is one of the few remaining downtown churches. It was designed by J.W. Yost in 1892, and its style—solid, stone Romanesque architecture—is reminiscent of that of H.H. Richardson.

English Lutheran Church, Knoxville, Tenn. Now known as St. John's Lutheran, this church is located at 544 North Broadway. It was given in 1912 by Mrs. Martha Henson in memory of her husband, and it was designed by R.F. Graf in Gothic Revival style.

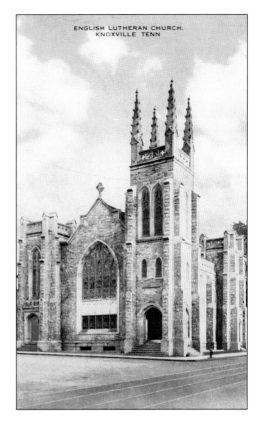

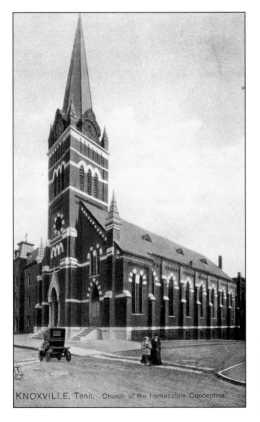

The Church of the Immaculate Conception, Knoxville, Tenn. This is one of downtown Knoxville's oldest buildings. Located on West Vine Avenue, it was designed by Joseph P. and Albert B. Baumann in 1884.

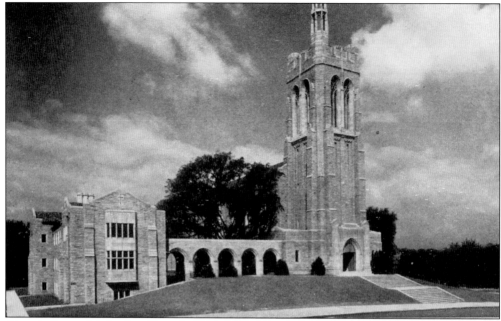

Church Street Methodist Church, Knoxville, Tenn. A modern Gothic church, located at 900 Henley Street, this building replaced an older church that had stood on Church Street. Erected in 1930 by John Russell Pope of New York and Barber and McMurry of Knoxville, it is considered one of the finest church buildings in the city.

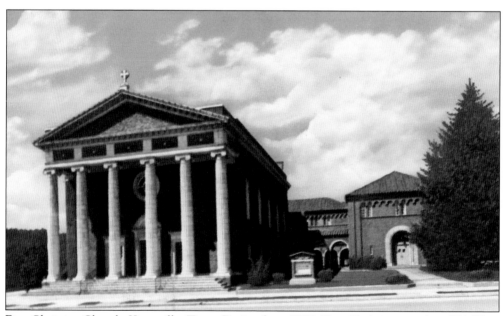

First Christian Church, Knoxville, Tenn. Dating from 1915, First Christian stands at 211 West Fifth Avenue. It has a monumental Ionic portico of terra cotta and brick. The wing that was added in 1929 was designed in Italian Romanesque style.

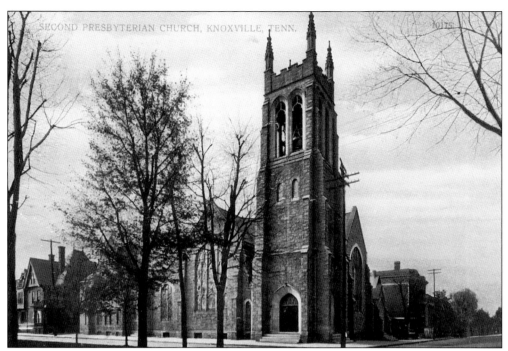

SECOND PRESBYTERIAN CHURCH, KNOXVILLE, TENN.

Second Presbyterian Church, Knoxville, Tenn. This structure was built in 1906 at the corner of Church and Walnut. The congregation has since moved to a Kingston Pike location.

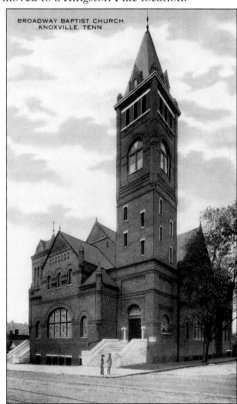

Broadway Baptist Church, Knoxville, Tenn. This building was completed in 1898. The postcard, mailed in 1916, reads: "Your card came. Sure glad to hear you are well again. Went out in a King car yesterday and had a fine time."

115

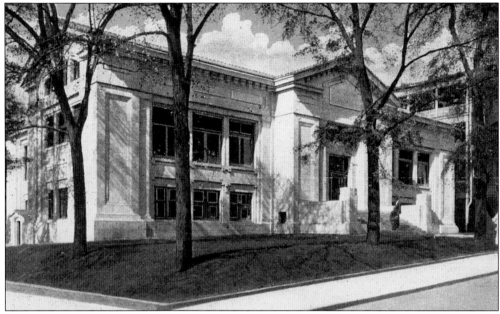

The Lawson McGhee Library, Knoxville, Tenn. Charles McClung McGhee established this library in 1885 as a memorial to his daughter, May Lawson McGhee Williams. This building at the corner of Market and Commerce appeared in 1917 and served the reading public for half a century.

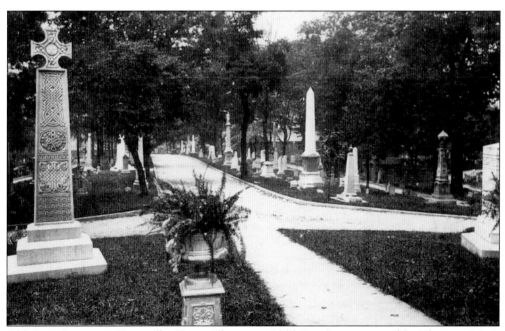

Old Gray Cemetery, Knoxville, Tenn. The name "Old Gray" was inspired by Thomas Gray's poem "Elegy in a Country Churchyard." Established in 1850, it contains many unique memorials to prominent people, including William G. Brownlow and L.D. Tyson.

Soldiers Monument, National Cemetery, Knoxville, Tenn. This tall memorial with a statue of a soldier on top dominates the National Cemetery. It memorializes the Union soldiers buried here.

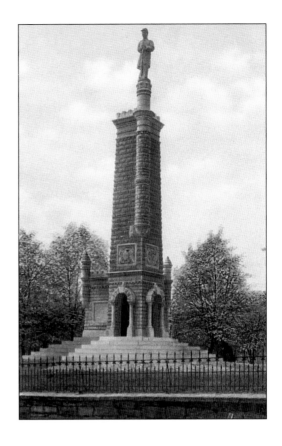

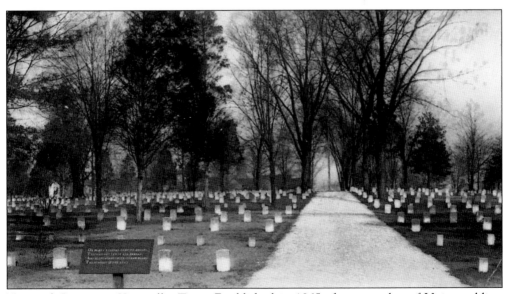

National Cemetery, Knoxville, Tenn. Established in 1865 after a number of Union soldiers were buried in Old Gray Cemetery (which is adjacent), this area was later expanded and given its own entrance on Tyson Street.

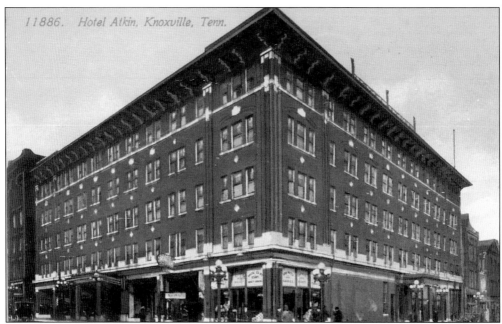

Hotel Atkin, Knoxville, Tenn. Just across the street from the Southern Railway Station, the Atkin was "just five minutes from the train," according to the publicity. Through the years it declined, along with railway passenger service; its space ultimately became a parking lot. The sender of this 1913 card writes: "Arrived in Knoxville Wed. morning and having a fine time. I've seen everything in Knoxville that's to be seen. ha Ha. How are you getting along in school? I got me a dandy new suit."

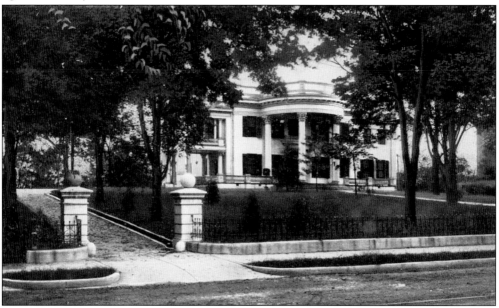

C.B. Atkin Residence, Knoxville, Tenn. The Clay Brown Atkin home stood at 518 West Main Street. It was originally the Perez Dickinson house, but was remodeled by George Barber in 1905. Splendid use was made of classical ornament in this building, including a Corinthian portico, which was saved when the house was demolished.

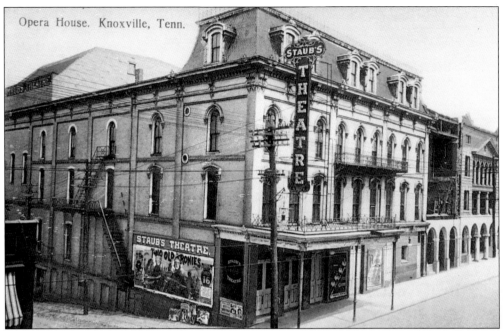

Opera House (Staub's Theatre), Knoxville, Tenn. This three-story brick building housed a popular theater for nearly 80 years. Located at Gay and Cumberland, it was built in 1872 by Peter Staub, a Swiss tailor who became one of Knoxville's most important businessmen. It seated 2,000 people and had a special gallery for blacks. Many important theatrical companies performed here. It became Loew's in 1920 and the name was changed to The Lyric in 1922.

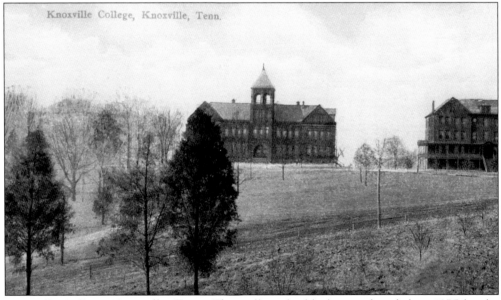

Knoxville College, Knoxville, Tenn. This college for blacks was founded in 1875 by the United Presbyterian Church as a grade and Normal school. In 1930 the preparatory division was closed. The correspondent, in 1911, is obviously a student: "The school now has about 400 students in all departments. I am enjoying my work of science and math and I expect to be here the whole year."

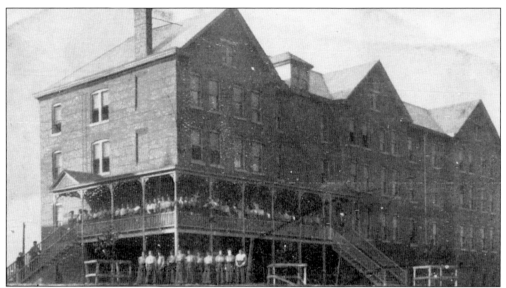

Elnathan Hall at Knoxville College, Knoxville, Tenn. We can tell that this card was made before 1907 by looking at the women's dress styles and by "address only" back of the card.

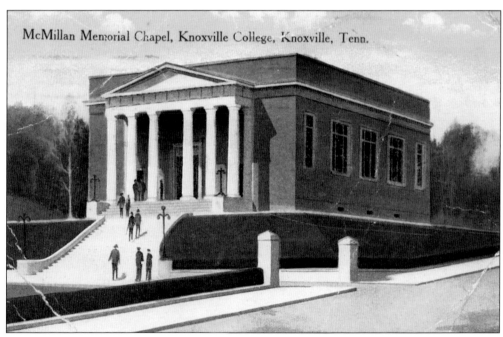

McMillan Memorial Chapel, Knoxville College, Knoxville, Tenn. Mailed in 1919, this card is from a student: "Hello, Prof. Mitchell, how are you? Ana and I are all well. Hope you and the school to be the same. How is all the students? Do you have a large number in school this year? I'm in the little girls' home down here—we have 52. In the large girls' home they have over 100. In the boys' home there is about 150. So we look like the whole Knoxville."

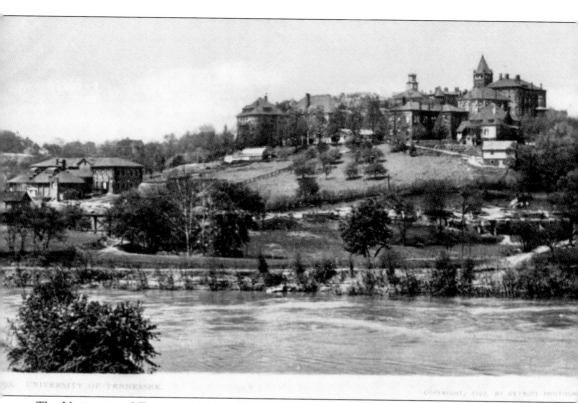

The University of Tennessee, Knoxville, Tenn. This long view of the UT campus from the south side shows why it is called "The Hill." Founded in 1794, the university looked like this about 1905.

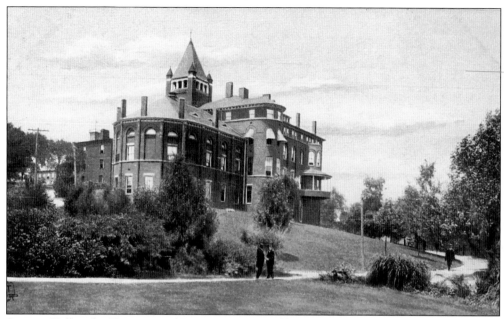

Science Hall at the University of Tennessee, Knoxville, Tenn. Built in 1892, Science Hall was one of the most beautiful buildings on campus. It contained an auditorium with a pipe organ and much beautiful interior craftsmanship.

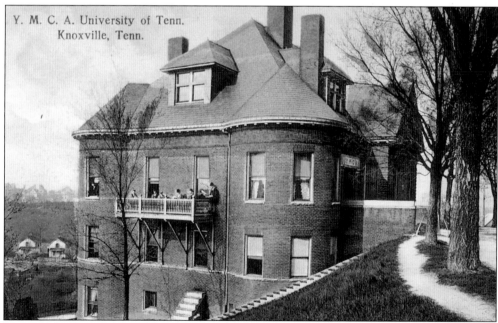

The Y.M.C.A., University of Tenn., Knoxville, Tenn. One of the first Y.M.C.A. chapters to be organized in a southern college, the UT chapter came to life in 1876; its building was begun in 1890. A favorite campus site for more than fifty years, it was demolished by fire in 1943.